SO BAD

It's Good

Edward Scimia

ISBN-10: 1479319880
EAN-13: 9781479319886

Table of Contents

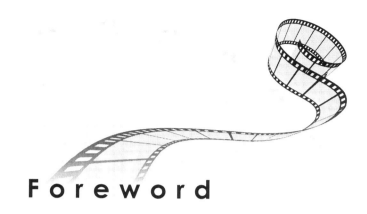

Foreword

Bad movies are good for you. If you don't believe that, you have to believe in yin and yang, good and evil, the Light and the Dark Side—or something or other. What I mean to say is, you can't have good movies without the bad, and sometimes it takes the very worst to show you the very best.

The most terrible thing a movie can do is be unremarkable. The kind of movie that is neither terrible nor good and ends up chucked into the limbo of Forgotten Films, where you end up losing an hour and half of your life. There's nothing to be gained there. Those are the films that disappoint me—the ones that squander their potential and simply exist to take up shelf space. To be truly great, a movie has to be either the very best or the very worst.

I haven't always loved terrible movies. This has been a fairly recent finding of mine. It started with a delightfully awful film called *Undefeatable*. That's when I discovered the concept of the so-bad-it's-good movie. I won't lie to you and say that *Undefeatable* is well-made or well-acted—it is, in fact, the opposite of those things. The lines are stilted, the villain is hilarious, and it's filled with so much mullet it deserved a starring credit. The final fight scene contains more grease than a KFC.

And it will blow you away.

The movie is incredibly funny. It may not have been intentional, but it's the saving grace of the film. That's why I love it. All I require from a motion picture is that it entertains me, and if I remember it, it's a step in the right direction. Sometimes a movie gets everything wrong and that's amazing. It's hard to imagine how the movie got made, and oftentimes, that's one of the most interesting parts about it. There's a story behind each and every one of these films—the DVDs you found in a dollar bin or the VHS that was left gathering dust at the closed down Blockbuster. Films are time capsules in that way, reminding us of a moment when those video stores still existed, when you could scan the shelves and see the glory of something called *Ninja Koala* or *Chainsaw Feet*. Sometimes the time capsule is in the movie itself, immortalizing the very worst of the trends that decade had to offer. It's a shared memory—whether it's with the filmmakers or the people you spend time with—you laugh, you cry, and you remember.

Not only is a bad film entertaining, it's a lesson in how not to make a movie. Because these films are usually made independently, a lot of things can go wrong—whether it be running out of budget or simply not having the talent to begin with. These filmmakers are learning as they go along and we learn with them. There are two ways a classic film is made: through sheer luck, or trial and error. By taking lessons from the movies that didn't have success, didn't make sense, or simply *didn't*, the good stuff becomes even better. We learn from failure. However, to label a movie that is so-bad-it's-good as a *failure* doesn't do it justice. It's the *best kind* of failure—a glorious train wreck of terrible lines, wobbling cameras, and shoddy effects. If a movie can transcend being awful and turn itself around, it's become a success.

Discovering B-movies has been an ongoing journey for me and I can tell you with every ounce of sincerity that I've discovered more laughter and richness in my life since that journey began. I've gained a more critical eye while embracing the films most people throw out. I also can't go to the theater and enjoy a movie in quite the same way, because I see things wrong that I couldn't see before. I don't see it as a loss, though. I can only be thankful that I can see these things now and it's *all* because of terrible movies. I'm no longer content to just accept being handed a big pile of horse manure—glossy as it may be. I need more substance in my life and that can't be a bad thing. I may have lost the ability to enjoy a big summer movie, but I've gained the ability to find the positive in the movies I used to dismiss. There are a lot of smaller films out there with merit and I find more satisfaction in watching those than the latest blockbuster. While the movies I see at the theater have all the budget, B-movies have more *heart*.

To make a movie on your own—ideas, money, or talent be damned—you have to have the drive and the belief in your product. A Hollywood film has so many hands in the pot, so many rewrites and re-edits, so much money on the line, that it's a miracle that anything comes out making sense in the end, much less a good movie. Truthfully, a successful film is almost always an accident, but bad movies are all about someone with a dream, someone who has a vision, and even if it's a terrible vision, it's one they get to share with the world. I can't hate something someone put so much earnestness into. I find myself rooting for them in all of their messy success.

The B-movie makers are the heroes of the world, and honestly, they've changed my life. I've shared so many laughs with good friends, met new people, and learned new things. I refuse to believe a movie can be *bad* if it's brought me that.

So thank you, Tommy Wiseau. Thank you, James Nguyen. Thank you, Sam Mraovich. Thank you, Godfrey Ho. Thank you, everyone. You put your hearts out on your sleeve and shared your horrible dreams with us and that means more than I can say.

If you take one thing away from this book, let it be this: There's more merit to a movie that *meant* something than a movie that's well-made. If you laughed, if you got angry, even if you were just confused, you got something out of it. Your world has changed, even if it's minutely, because you've gained something from the experience. I suppose, in that respect, there's no such thing as a bad movie.

-*Allison Pregler*
Obscurus Lupa, z-grade movie fan,
and sometimes comedian

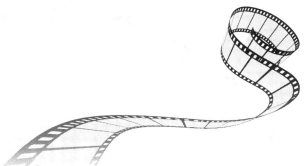

Acknowledgements

Where to begin? I'd like to thank Allison Pregler, not only for contributing her many thoughts on the subject of bad movies, but also for her efforts in spreading the word about this project when it was in its infancy. If you're a fan of B-movies, you owe it to yourself to take a look at Allison's web series *Obscurus Lupa Presents* on ThatGuyWithTheGlasses.com or Phelous.com.

Another big thank you goes out to Douglas Fox, Andrew Joyce, James Lasome, and Patrick Stergos, all of who contributed their thoughts to this book, along with pledging toward the Kickstarter project that made publishing the book possible.

I also need to thank the many other individuals who made significant pledges toward this book's Kickstarter, including, but not limited to: Ryan Alarie, Andrew G. Bene, Sarah Bengston, Jason Bourgeois, Adam Buckheit, Ricardo Arredondo Casso, Johnny Caps, Matt Clancy, Prairie Rose Clayton, Zackary Collins, Rachel Cordone, Karl Dahlberg, Darren Davis, Ryan Fletcher, William S. Gadaleta, Jeff Gilbert, Jake Hare, Hunter Harrell, James F. Ilika, Dan Jedrejczyk, Maria Maravilla Juárez, Nate Kirby, Ammar Khalid, Will King, Bri Lafond, Paul Leone, Jim

Lesniak, Sian Lloyd-Wiggins, Alexander Lowson, Ed Matuskey, Graeme McGaw, Joe McLaughlin, Mark D. Montgomery II, Greg Nowacki, Anthony Pizzo, L. Ross Raszewski, Jen Sander, David Alan Scott Jr., Brad Shelton, Ryan J. Smith, Niall J.D. Somerville, Julia Steincross, Cody Stier, Mireille Suzaku, John Tsentzelis, Marissa Wilk, Bryan "WinterWarlock" Wilkes, and Patrick "Psuedo-Otaku" Yee.

Finally, a thanks to the many friends who have watched more terrible movies with me than anyone could reasonably be asked to sit through. I'd especially like to thank Margaret Broz, Hollysdower, Kassamai, Michael Knight, Adam Lasik, Abby Root, and Chris Taylor—each of who survived the unenviable task of watching both animated Titanic films back-to-back in a single night.

Introduction:
Plan 9 from Outer Space

In the world of film, there are timeless classics that virtually everyone agrees are worth watching. *The Godfather*, *Casablanca*, and *Citizen Kane* may not be your cup of tea, but few people would deny that any of these movies don't belong on any list of the greatest films ever created. These movies were made by talented individuals, both behind and in front of the camera, resulting in works of art that entertain us, touch us emotionally, and make us think.

This book is not about those movies.

While most moviegoers can appreciate a truly great film, it takes a certain type of person to love a movie that's so bad, it's good. You have to be willing to accept a little bit of pain along with your pleasure. You need to find beauty in terrible line reads, lazy writing, and cheesy special effects. It takes at least a small amount of *schadenfreude*—that special kind of pleasure that comes from watching the failure of others.

If you want to enjoy a bad movie, you'll need to have a healthy sense of humor. While a good movie derives its entertainment value from a thrilling storyline, fantastic performances, or stunning cinematography, you can't expect to get any of those from a bad movie. On their faces, bad movies offer very little to the viewer—at least in traditional terms—but when a movie manages to fail on multiple levels, it can become funny in ways the creators never intended. It's this unintentional humor that gives a "good" bad movie its irresistible charm.

I could write a few paragraphs explaining what exactly makes a movie so bad, it's good, but it's much easier to do that if we have an example to work from. With that in mind, let's take a look at what might just be the prototypical enjoyably bad film—a true classic that set the standard by which all other bad films are judged.

PLAN 9 FROM OUTER SPACE
DIRECTED BY EDWARD WOOD JR.
REYNOLDS PICTURES (1959)

Plan 9 from Outer Space probably isn't the worst movie ever made. While it's certainly very bad, I'd say it's not even a real contender for that title. However, if *Plan 9* hadn't been given that designation in the 1980 book *The Golden Turkey Awards*, this Ed Wood film might have been forgotten and the world would be much worse off for it.

The plot of the film isn't so out of place for the science fiction fare of the era. In *Plan 9*, aliens come to Earth in an attempt to stop human scientists from continuing to develop more powerful weapons. They fear that the human race will eventually discover the secret of solarbonite—an element that can be used to create a bomb that will explode sunlight itself, destroying the entire universe.

Two aliens come to Earth in order to prevent this from occurring: Eros (Dudley Manlove) and Tanna (Joanna Lee). They use an alien device to resurrect three humans who recently died: a couple played by Bela Lugosi and Vampira, as well as a very strong police officer, Inspector Clay (Tor Johnson). Meanwhile, the government and military are growing concerned about increasing UFO reports in California, as well as messages they've intercepted from the aliens, and dispatch Colonel Edwards (Tom Keene) to investigate.

The alien-controlled zombies terrorize locals, who soon discover that they are virtually unstoppable,as gunfire does nothing to even slow them down. Eventually, the aliens lure much of the cast aboard their spaceship, where they explain their concerns with the direction of human technological advancement. A fight aboard the ship ultimately leads to a fire, which kills the aliens and deactivating the zombies and ends the extraterrestrial threat.

That short summary should give you the idea that *Plan 9 from Outer Space* isn't a very good movie. But what sets it apart from a thousand other not-so-great films that aren't going to show up in this book? Here's a quick rundown of a few of the elements that make *Plan 9* such a classic of the genre. Not all of the movies in this book will share all of these qualities, but it's almost certain that no movie found itself in here without at least a few of these.

BAD WRITING

Terrible writing—particularly when it comes to the dialogue spoken on screen—is a common feature of enjoyable bad movies. After all, a bad line or two isn't just something to laugh at. Long after the movie is over, you can quote those lines for additional laughs with other fans of the movie, or use them as examples of exactly why the movie is so bad when talking to those who have never seen it.

In the case of *Plan 9*, absurd writing can be found everywhere. One of the most obvious examples comes from The Amazing Criswell, the narrator of the film. During the introduction to the movie Criswell tells viewers: "future events such as these will affect you in the future." At the end of the film, Criswell tells us: "My friend, you have seen this incident, based on sworn testimony. Can you prove that it didn't happen?" Indeed we can't, Criswell.

The dialogue spoken by characters throughout the film isn't much better. Speaking of how the government attempted to contact the aliens but failed, Colonel Edwards tells us that the aliens "attacked a town: a small town I'll admit, but never the less a town of people. People who died." The aliens don't fare any better. When Tanna (the female in the alien duo) starts to argue their case for destroying Earth in order to save the universe, Eros shoves her and tells her to stop and explains: "in my land, women are for advancing the race, not for fighting man's battles."

BAD ACTING

If our first element is all about what's contained in the script, this second feature of bad films is all about how the cast interprets and delivers what was given to them. Some movies suffer because actors could do little with a bad script, while others are decent in concept, but are strangled by talent that either deliver their lines with a dull flatness or decide to show off their "passion" through melodramatic overacting. Often, a great bad movie will combine these two elements, giving us terrible dialogue that's delivered terribly.

While *Plan 9* has far from an all-star cast, the acting is probably the least of its sins. Oh, it certainly has its moments: Eros screams at his human adversaries and one actor is clearly reading his lines off a script sitting in his lap. Clearly, most of the cast wasn't heavily invested in the film, so their delivery is often wooden. But in a film where most areas would be rated a zero on a one to ten scale, most of the principals at least give enough of an effort to earn the acting a 1.5.

POOR PRODUCTION VALUES

This area can cover a variety of different issues, and generally relates to how things are presented to the viewing audience. Perhaps the sets and costumes are poorly designed, or the editing is confusing. It can even be something as simple as the relatively common error of allowing the boom mic to be seen. In any case, this is an area where it can quickly become apparent that the filmmakers weren't quite up to the task of creating a high-quality film—usually because of a lack of money or skill and often both.

Plan 9 is infamous for these sorts of issues. Flying saucers are clearly suspended on wires that are all too visible, headstones in a graveyard are easily knocked over by falling actors, and scenes frequently change between day and night from shot to shot. Some shots feature actors who are clearly against backdrops, which is made all the more obvious when you can see their shadows against the "sky."

THE X–FACTOR

All of the above factors are important, and often they're sufficient to make a bad film enjoyable, but to truly become a legendary bad movie, there has to be something more. Perhaps it's a particular scene that's so bad you'll never forget it. It could be an aspect of the plot that's absolutely ludicrous. Sometimes, it's a fault in the filmmaking process, like terrible animation or horrific sound.

In the case of *Plan 9*, the X-Factor is one Bela Lugosi. While *Plan 9 from Outer Space* was released in 1959, primary filming for the movie took place mainly in 1956—the same year that Lugosi passed away. Director Ed Wood was keen on using the legendary Lugosi in a number of different films, but none of those projects had been completed. However, he had filmed several scenes with Lugosi in them and Wood couldn't imagine letting those precious frames go to waste.

The result was that several scenes of Lugosi were placed in *Plan 9*, even though they had nothing to do with anything in the script. In order to make this work, Lugosi's segments were tied to a character that would ultimately be portrayed in all other scenes by Tom Mason—a chiropractor used by Wood's wife. In order to maintain the illusion that Lugosi was present throughout the film, Mason played his part with a cape covering the lower half of his face. The idea was to make Mason unrecognizable from Lugosi, but there were several issues with this—not the least of which were that Mason was noticeably taller and in no way resembled Lugosi. Nonetheless, using the other footage allowed Lugosi to be credited in the film, which ultimately led to his guest star billing, despite the fact that he was hardly in the film at all.

SINCERITY

One final factor that can never be overlooked is the sincere effort that has been put into the production of a film. A truly great bad movie can't be forced. It has to be the result of a director's legitimate attempt to make a good film and coming up short. When someone tries to make a bad film on purpose, it's usually painfully obvious, and not nearly as fun as the genuine article.

No matter what anyone says about his work, there's no doubting that Ed Wood was nothing if sincere in his attempts to make good movies. Wood loved his films, from *Glen or Glenda*—a serious look at the life of a transvestite—to *Plan 9*, which he referred to as his "pride and joy." Although Wood may not have had the talent to be a great director, he refused to stop even when his own financial situation became dire. He was clearly a man who loved film and threw himself into every film he made full force.

It's this level of effort and sincerity that makes *Plan 9 from Outer Space* not only a must watch for all bad movie fans, but also the perfect example of what it takes to make a bad movie fun. If you're going to call yourself a bad movie fan, there's no getting around watching *Plan 9*.

About This Book

In the pages to follow, you'll find a wide selection of some of my favorite so bad, they're good movies. In the first chapter—Bad Movies 101—you'll find some of the other bad movie classics that are right up there with *Plan 9* as movies that all bad movie fans have to see. After that, I've tried to divide the remaining choices thematically, so if there are certain types of films you like—or can't stand—you can quickly find movies relevant to you. At the end of the book, you'll find some recommendations from other bad movie experts and fans, as well as a few honorable mentions that might also be worth a look. Many entries include additional information after the general summary of the movie, divided into topics like Fun Facts, What to Watch For, and Related Films.

I feel it's important to note that this book is in no way a definitive collection of bad movies. There are hundreds, maybe even thousands, of bad movies that can be fun to watch under the right circumstances. The movies covered in this book were my own personal selections, but they should only serve as a jumping off point for your own adventures in unintentionally hilarious cinema. It's also important to realize that everyone's tastes are different, and that there very well might be a couple films in here that you think are legitimately good. That's okay. To be honest, I love a few of the movies in this book, but feel like they're guilty pleasures—or at least the kinds of films that bad movie fans are likely to enjoy.

I hope you'll discover some great new bad movies thanks to this book. Sit back and enjoy the show!

Bad Movies 101

When it comes to watching enjoyable, terrible cinema, everyone has to start somewhere. Over the years, the genre has developed to the point where there are a handful of classics that every bad movie fan has seen. This chapter shines the spotlight on those films and should give those looking to get into the world of bad movies a great place to start.

In the process of writing this book, I talked to many reviewers and fans. One of the common questions I asked of them was, if you had to introduce someone to the joy of bad movies, and they had never tried watching a fun-bad movie before, what movie would you choose?

The answers were varied, but almost inevitably, the movies chosen were among the most infamous bad movies ever produced. In the end, one movie was recommended far more than any other: *Troll 2*.

"*Troll 2* is consistently hilarious all throughout the movie," says Douglas Fox, a longtime fan of terrible films. "Every actor, scene, and special effect combines into glorious *badness*. There is never a dull moment."

"It's just such an absolute classic in that subgenre," James "Crypticsych" Lasome of Best-Horror-Movies.com told me. "They'd know immediately after watching it whether they'd want to keep digging."

You'll find *Troll 2* in this chapter, but it's hardly the only so bad, it's good masterpiece that deserves a mention. Aside from the aforementioned *Plan 9 from Outer Space*, the most famously popular bad movie of all time might just be *The Room*—the 2003 Tommy Wiseau film that has likely inspired more midnight showings than any movie since *The Rocky Horror Picture Show*.

"The best of the best has to be *The Room*," says Allison Pregler, who has reviewed the Wiseau classic and countless other B-movies in her web series *Obscurus Lupa Presents*. "It's obvious from start to finish that this movie hasn't got a hope or a prayer of picking itself up out of its hold of mediocrity and it's glorious to watch the ship continue to sink. There are constant dropped subplots, random bursts of ridiculous or nonsensical dialogue, and it is a wonderful starter movie for those folks looking to get into the guilty pleasure culture."

The films that follow are those classics that have risen above the typical bad film. These are the movies that have something that makes them appeal to wider audience, even those who wouldn't normally go out of their way in order to watch a bad movie. Some of these movies have been around for decades, while others are relative newcomers, but one thing is for certain: if you're a true fan of movies that are so bad, they're good, you've seen them all.

TROLL 2
DIRECTED BY CLAUDIO FRAGASSO
FILMIRAGE (1990)

There's no doubt that *Troll 2* is one of the most famous bad movies ever—as well as one of the more entertaining. It's hard to point to any one element that has made this movie such a classic. Instead, it's the culmination of an unlikely set of circumstances that managed to produce a film that's both horrendously bad and undeniably enjoyable.

The first thing you'll notice when watching *Troll 2* is that there aren't any trolls involved. The film's antagonists are gob-lins, which is why the movie was originally titled *Goblins*. But distributors feared that the movie wouldn't spark enough interest on its own, so they gave it the title *Troll 2* in an attempt to tie it to an earlier film by the name of *Troll*. This was a curious deci-sion in its own right. While *Troll* had its fans and managed to turn a profit, it was far from a mainstream hit, and four years had passed since its release.

On the other hand, it's easy to see why they thought *Troll 2* would need a little help to catch on with audiences. The movie tells the story of the Waits family, who have decided to take their summer vacation in a small town named Nilbog. But some-thing is amiss—the family's youngest member, Joshua (Michael Stephenson) is warned by the ghost of his grandfather (Robert

Ormsby) that evil goblins will soon put his whole family in grave danger. The rest of the family—father/Michael (George Hardy), mother/Diane (Margo Prey) and sister/Holly (Connie McFarland)—assumes that Joshua is imagining these conversations, like a slightly creepier version of having an imaginary friend.

Joshua's warnings are ignored, and the family travels to Nilbog for their rustic vacation. Also along for the journey is Holly's boyfriend, Elliot (Jason Wright), who goes with the family in order to prove his love for Holly. However, Elliot also brought three of his friends—Arnold (Darren Ewing), Brent (David McConnell), and Drew (Jason Steadman)—along to keep him company. The four of them share an RV parked just outside of the town.

Despite plenty of visions and warnings along the way, Joshua can't stop his family from arriving in Nilbog, where they're greeted by the first of many feasts left for them by the town's residents. This is no ordinary feast, however—it's entirely made up of vegetables and some of the food seems to be just a little *too* green. Once again, Joshua sees his grandfather, who tells him that the food is poisoned and will turn them into vegetable people who will then be devoured by the people of Nilbog, who are actually goblins.

Grandpa stops time for thirty seconds in order to give Joshua a chance to prevent his family from eating the food by any means necessary. Joshua tries to come up with a plan, but time is running out and he's flush out of ideas. At the final moment, he manages to think of the most brilliant and elegant solution available: he urinates all over the table, ruining the food.

Make no mistake: *Troll 2* is a bad movie even before the pee-ing scene, but that's right around when it becomes clear that this is no ordinary bad movie, and that you're probably in for a real treat. Thankfully, this is one film that doesn't know when to quit.

Next up is one of the most infamous scenes in bad movie history. Elliot's friend, Arnold, is walking in the woods when he runs into a scared woman being chased by goblins. After trying to scare them off—Arnold doesn't prove to be very frightening—the two run to the apparent safety of a chapel. There, they find a very strange woman by the name of Creedence Leonore Gielgud (Deborah Reed), who feeds them some of the same substance that was left for the Waits family. It turns out that Creedence is the druid queen and leader of the goblins. It's already too late to escape, though. Arnold is stuck as a half-man, half-plant abomi-nation, while the young woman he saved earlier has already turned into gooey plant matter. The goblins arrive and begin eating what's left of the girl, leading Arnold to deliver a line that has been viewed millions of times on YouTube: "They're eating her. And then they're going to eat me! Oh my God!".

The rest of the film mainly consists of the residents of Nilbog attempting to get the Waits family to eat food that will turn them into edible plant creatures. They try parties, they try leav-ing food around the house, and they even try to get family mem-bers to eat food sold in the town's only store—but nothing works, as Joshua constantly manages to thwart their plans while his parents refuse to listen to his pleas, despite mounting evidence that things in Nilbog are not all that they seem.

Eventually, the town preacher is killed, causing him to turn into his true goblin form. This is finally enough to get the family's attention, and they barricade themselves in their house in order to defend against the goblin townspeople. After summoning the grandfather once more through a séance, Joshua receives the ultimate weapon that will lead to the goblins' defeat: a bologna sandwich. No, really.

That plot summary has probably left you with more than a few questions, not the least of which are "how?" and "why?" Well, it's time for me to fess up: I left out a few key details that allow some insight into exactly how *Troll 2* came to be.

Troll 2 was the work of director Claudio Fragasso and his wife Rosella Drudi, an Italian couple who didn't have full command of the English language. Drudi was actually responsible for the initial story idea, which came to her after she felt frustrated by many of her friends, who had become vegetarians. The story was, in her eyes, a great way to express her feelings about their dietary habits.

That explains the plot, but it's only the beginning of the *Troll 2* story. The film would ultimately be shot in Utah, and after a short casting call—which resulted in many of the roles going to non-actors who had simply hoped to have some fun and possibly be cast as extras—filming began in the summer of 1989.

Immediately, the production had some serious issues. Most of the crew spoke Italian, with only a single fluent English speaker—outside of the cast—on set for most of the production. This led to great confusion and a general lack of communication between cast and crew, with many cast members reporting that they rarely had much of an idea of what was going on. The script was written in broken English, and while the actors tried to modify it as much as possible, several have said that Fragasso wouldn't allow them to do so—a claim the director disputes.

Despite all of this, *Troll 2* certainly isn't one of the worst movies ever made. In fact, it's probably not even one of the worst movies in this book. The technical aspects of the film are quite competent, and unlike some of the first-time directors whose movies become infamous for being terrible, Fragasso had already directed more than ten films by the time *Troll 2* was filmed. The goblin costumes are terrible—the movie doesn't even try to hide the fact that the actors are just wearing masks—and the score is boring, but those are typical problems for a low-budget film.

Troll 2 has earned its legacy because it strikes almost the perfect balance necessary for bad movie enjoyment. It's terrible, but not so bad as to become painful. The plot is ridiculous, but it moves along at a fast enough pace so that you won't get bored. The dialogue is stupid and the performances are *legendarily* bad, but in a way that makes the worst lines quotable and the actors highly memorable.

In short, *Troll 2* is one of the worst films ever made that still remains highly watchable. You'll laugh at the absurdity of it all, but you're unlikely to wonder how much more of it you have to sit through or beg for it to come to a conclusion. It's a formula that's hard to replicate, and something that can probably only be achieved by accident.

WHAT TO WATCH FOR

- This film plays fast and loose with continuity, with many lines making little sense because of it. One of the earliest examples comes when the family arrives in Nilbog: Michael says that nobody is there to greet them, because everyone is asleep at that time of night, despite the fact that the entire scene takes place in unambiguously bright daylight.
- If you haven't experienced it, the aforementioned "Oh my God!" scene is a must see, either during the movie or as a standalone clip.
- *Nilbog* is *goblin* spelled backward! Sorry for the spoiler.
- Holly does a dance in front of a mirror that will go down in the annals of bad movie dances as one of the all-time greats.
- Another famous scene features Brent being seduced by Creedence, who has transformed into a beautiful woman. I don't want to give too much away, but this has widely become known as the "corn porn scene." Get your popcorn ready!

FUN FACTS

- George Hardy, who played Michael Waits, was a practicing dentist in Salt Lake City at the time the film was made, and was one of the many cast members who had expected only to be an extra in the film. Hardy is still a dentist to this day, and is now working in Alexander City, Alabama. He did not appear in another film for almost two decades.

- A more unusual casting story is that of Don Packard. According to Packard, he was in and out of mental hospitals at the time the film was being made, and happened to be out when he auditioned for the film. He would end up playing Nilbog's store owner, and claims that his disturbed performance had nothing to do with acting—it was a reflection of what he was like at that time in his life.

RELATED FILMS

- If you enjoy *Troll 2*, you must watch *Best Worst Movie*, a documentary that chronicles the making of *Troll 2*, as well as its recent popularity as a cult favorite. In contrast to *Troll 2*, *Best Worst Movie* has received excellent reviews and provides plenty of insights into how the film was made and what has become of much of the cast and crew.

THE ROOM
DIRECTED BY TOMMY WISEAU
TPW FILMS, WISEAU–FILMS, CHLOE
PRODUCTIONS (2003)

If you have any interest in bad movies at all, chances are you've at least heard whispers of *The Room*—the 2003 independent film by Tommy Wiseau. While some have described it as a contender for the worst film ever made, I don't think that's fair: there are far worse films mentioned in this book, and many more that are simply unwatchable and have been lost or forgotten by fans of terrible cinema. One thing is for sure, though—you will never, ever forget *The Room* once you've had the pleasure of viewing it.

It's hard to know how to begin discussing this film, so let's start with a little bit of background. *The Room* is the brainchild of Tommy Wiseau—a self-identified American with a strange and difficult-to-place European accent. In 2001, he first wrote *The Room* as a play, which he then adapted into a book. Having found no success in either of these formats, Wiseau decided that perhaps his vision could best be achieved through film.

That's where the story starts to get weird. Wiseau managed to raise six million dollars for his film, though he has yet to come clean about how exactly he managed to do this. He was determined to take complete and total control of the project, which led to him writing, directing, producing, and starring in *The Room*.

As one might expect, the production didn't go smoothly. Most of the cast and crew were replaced—often multiple times—and the script was apparently so bad that cast members were often editing their lines right up until the moment their scenes were filmed. That might be hard to believe when you sit down to watch the movie, but yes, at some point, the writing was even worse. Better still, Wiseau wasn't certain about whether to shoot the movie on thirty-five millimeter film or in high-definition video, and came up with an interesting solution—he shot it in both formats, using a dolly that could accommodate both cameras.

The Room is intended to be a drama about a banker from San Francisco named Johnny (Tommy Wiseau) who is struggling to maintain his relationship with his fiancée, Lisa (Juliette Danielle), who may have feelings for Johnny's best friend, Mark (Greg Sestero). It's a simple premise, but there's nothing wrong with a straightforward plot, right?

Oh, if only it were that easy. Throughout *The Room*, secondary characters—such as Denny (Phillip Haldiman), Lisa's mother, Claudette (Carolyn Minnott), and psychologist Peter (Kyle Vogt)—are constantly given plot lines that are introduced dramatically, but then never referenced again later in the film. This includes one infamous scene in which Caludette announces, "I definitely have breast cancer," which is never again mentioned.

The film also includes a number of...quirks. For instance, it seems that the men of *The Room*'s universe enjoy tossing the pigskin, but only from a distance of a few feet. Characters constantly enter rooms to speak a couple of lines then immediately leave. Johnny feels the need to greet every person he meets with, "Oh, hi—" followed with the name of the individual in question.

Then there are the film's five extended "love scenes." These sex scenes each come equipped with generic R&B music, lots of slow-motion camera work, and plenty of filters and effects presumably designed to give the scenes a more artistic feel. These are awkward affairs, to say the least—and with most of them clocking in at several minutes long, viewers are sure to get more than their fill of seeing Wiseau sans clothing.

The movie premiered at two Los Angeles theaters in June 2003. It was a colossal flop, making under two thousand dollars over two weeks before both theaters pulled it from their lineups. However, that was long enough for a few audience members to realize that they were watching a masterpiece of unintentional hilarity.

We should all be thankful that they did. This led to a series of midnight showings in Los Angeles, which helped *The Room* gain a reputation as an amazing cinematic experience—perhaps not in the way that Wiseau initially intended, but an experience nonetheless. Hollywood celebrities began spreading the word, and the movie even received a few mentions on the television series *Veronica Mars*.

Before long, *The Room* had become a cult phenomenon, with screenings being staged in theaters around the world. Today, audiences interact with the film every bit as much as you'd see at a showing of *The Rocky Horror Picture Show*, and at selected screenings, you might even get the honor of speaking to Wiseau himself.

The bottom line is that *The Room* is one of the most entertaining bad movies ever created. If you haven't had the honor of seeing it yourself, it's well worth either picking up a copy to show at your next bad movie night, or by finding a screening near you. Both options have their merits: at a live screening, you might get to throw plastic spoons at the screen, while the DVD comes with a question and answer session with Wiseau himself that does little to give viewers more insight into the film, but adds a few more minutes of positively Wiseau-ian entertainment.

WHAT TO WATCH FOR

- Almost every single line of dialogue. It's hard to give some of the best examples without spoiling the most quotable moments of the film, but the majority of lines spoken throughout the film range from slightly off to downright bizarre.
- The flower shop scene has become a favorite among fans. Although it is only twenty seconds long, it is filled with enough incomprehensible dialogue and strange sound editing that you're likely to immediately rewind and watch it a second time.
- Take a close look at the artwork and photos in Johnny's apartment. You'll find a number of strange choices— none more interesting than what appears to be a framed photograph of a spoon.
- The character of Peter mysteriously disappears late in the film, after which a new, nameless character shows up to deliver lines that seem to have clearly been meant for Peter. The story behind this is that Kyle Vogt only had a limited time to film his scenes, but Wiseau and the production team did not choose to shoot those scenes earlier. When he left, the rest of his lines were given to Greg Ellery.
- Did you know that this film takes place in San Francisco? Don't worry, it won't let you forget. There are several minutes worth of stock footage of the city included in the final cut.

BIRDEMIC: SHOCK AND TERROR
DIRECTED BY JAMES NGUYEN
MOVIEHEAD PICTURES (2008)

Birdemic: Shock and Terror is a true labor of love. Written, directed, and produced by James Nguyen, this was largely a one-man project, created without the help of a studio or even significant financing from investors. Not surprisingly, this didn't do wonders for the quality of the film. Despite having been released recently, it has already garnered a reputation as one of the worst films ever made.

The plot of *Birdemic* centers on Rod (Alan Bagh) and Nathalie (Whitney Moore), a couple who spend the first half of the film inexplicably falling in love. Rod is a software salesman who dreams of starting a green technology company, while Nathalie is an aspiring model who apparently works out of a one-hour photo store. Both achieve remarkably quick success in their respective careers while also finding plenty of time to develop their blossoming relationship.

Then, the birds attack.

The attack scene is one of the most infamous in recent bad movie history, as exploding birds seem to set most of a city on fire. These avian wonders generate the kinds of sounds one would expect to hear from military bombers rather than eagles. For the rest of the film, Rod and Nathalie frantically search for safety in the face of continuous bird attacks.

The plot itself may well be enough to convince you that this is a truly awful—yet enjoyable—film, but that's just the tip of the iceberg. It's hard to overstate just how poor the production values on in *Birdemic*. There's bizarre sound editing, plenty of laughable CGI, and dialogue that's as poorly delivered as it is written. Some scenes go on for far too long, while others are cut off abruptly. *Birdemic* tries to deliver an arguably important environmental message, but it's hard to take it seriously when the amateurish production overshadows any lessons the movie expected to impart on its audience.

Despite these shortcomings, *Birdemic* somehow remains watchable—if only as something to laugh at. *Birdemic* is bad, but it is never boring. Whether you're questioning the increasingly poor decisions being made by the characters, mocking the stilted conversations, or wondering aloud about the film's many plot holes, *Birdemic* never stops providing material for you and your friends to riff on. Besides, the first appearance of the birds alone makes this movie worthwhile: everything else is just gravy.

FUN FACTS

- *Birdemic* was reportedly created on a budget of less than ten thousand dollars. Once you've seen the film, this isn't terribly difficult to believe.
- Both *The Birds* and *An Inconvenient Truth* have been acknowledged as inspirations for *Birdemic*. This is pretty

clear from the subject matter of the film itself, but just to make it clear, *Birdemic* includes references to both films: Tippi Hedren appears on a television set, while the characters have an awkward conversation that tells us how impressed they were by Al Gore's documentary.

- Say what you will about the film itself, but Nguyen certainly went above and beyond in his efforts to promote this movie. In 2009, Nguyen traveled to the Sundance Film Festival and handed out fliers from his van to raise buzz about *Birdemic*. Sure, he may have misspelled the title of his own website, and the grammar of the signs left something to be desired—some are said to have read "WHY DID THE EAGLES AND VULTURES ATTACKED?"—but the work paid off. After a local screening, *Birdemic* began building a reputation—though probably not the one Nguyen intended.

WHAT TO WATCH FOR

- The opening scene should clue you into the fact that *Birdemic* has a few pacing issues. If you enjoy watching people drive slowly on rather ordinary roads, you'll be enthralled!
- There's a nice musical interlude in the middle of the film that is guaranteed to get stuck in your head for days. "Just hangin' out, hangin' out, hangin' out with my family..."
- With a name like *Birdemic*, it goes without saying that the birds steal the show. This film teaches us that birds

16

have a number of special abilities they rarely use in our world: hovering in place, exploding upon impact with just about any object, and in one scene even releasing some sort of deadly acid. These CGI creations really have to be seen to be believed. If you're not convinced, you can find numerous clips of the birds in action on the internet, but it's even more fun if you're introduced to them during the movie.

- When birds attack, it's always important to arm yourself. Preferably with coat hangers.
- Remember, when trying to save people trapped on a bus from a bird attack, you should always practice proper gun safety. In the *Birdemic* universe, this means that you will want to fire directly at the birds hovering in front of the bus, as this will do no damage to either the vehicle or the people watching through its windows.
- Late in the movie, our characters run into a very Tommy Wiseau-like character that lives in harmony with nature in the woods. This scene is notable not only for the ham-fisted speech delivered by this character—certainly not the film's first—but also for the CGI fire and the dramatic inclusion of a mountain lion.
- Almost every other moment in this film.

RELATED FILMS

If this movie leaves you wanting more exploding bird action, you won't have to wait long. *Birdemic II: The Resurrection* is slated for a fall 2012 release, and promises to deliver more of the same for *Birdemic* fans. Both of the leads will return for the sequel, which is said to center on a bird attack in Hollywood. Best of all, the sequel will reportedly be available in 3D, meaning you'll be able to watch eagles and vultures hovering right in front of your face!

Also, while *Birdemic* is certainly James Nguyen's most famous film, it is not his only work. True fans of his unique style will also want to check out *Julie and Jack* (2003), a classic Nguyen film that features many of the same issues as his later work—only without the CGI birds.

GYMKATA
DIRECTED BY ROBERT CLOUSE
MGM (1985)

There's no doubt that gymnasts deserve a lot of respect. If you've ever watched gymnastics during the Olympics, you're well aware that these athletes do things with their bodies that seem virtually impossible, and somehow manage to stay balanced and keep smiles on their faces at the same time. Given these amazing talents, it's no surprise that a film studio might try to take advantage of these abilities.

That was likely the thought process that led to *Gymkata*. This film stars one of the most successful American gymnasts of the

1970s, Kurt Thomas. In *Gymkata*, Thomas plays the role of an Olympic gymnast named Jonathan Cabot. Obviously, it's a role that should suit an actual gymnast—indeed, Thomas has plenty of opportunities to show that his gymnastics skills were still top notch at the time the movie was filmed—but it's where *Gymkata* takes this character that makes this film a favorite of bad movie aficionados.

Cabot is recruited by an agency that is certainly not the CIA to play "the Game" on behalf of the United States government. In order to compete in this Game, Cabot will have to travel to the tiny, backward, and fictional country of Parmistan. The government hopes that Cabot can win the Game, as any winner can request one wish of Parmistan's king. The United States would like to place a satellite monitoring station in the country, and apparently has no better way of accomplishing this than sending a gymnast. Before he can go, however, Cabot must learn how to combine his gymnastics skills with traditional martial arts, creating an all-new fighting style known as gymkata.

Once Cabot arrives in Parmistan, he learns a little more about the Game. It's essentially a giant obstacle course, during which ninjas shoot arrows at the contestants. Oh, there are apparently rules dictating when and how they can fire the arrows, but the enforcement of these regulations is somewhat inconsistent. Only if a contestant can survive each stage of the Game and make it back to the capital alive can they be crowned winner.

Reading this summary, you might guess that Thomas himself was one of the major issues with *Gymkata*. Actually, he turns in a respectable performance, particularly when compared to most other athlete-to-actor transitions. In fact, unlike many of the movies in this book, bad acting isn't a major factor in its inclusion. Instead, you'll spend your time laughing at the ridiculous premise and the goofy fight scenes that have made *Gymkata* famous.

FUN FACTS

- While Kurt Thomas was undoubtedly a great gymnast, he never actually won a medal at the Olympics. Thomas won two gold medals and three silver medals in the 1979 World Championships, firmly placing him among the top male gymnasts in the world. Unfortunately for Thomas, the United States boycotted the 1980 Summer Olympics in Moscow, denying him the opportunity at Olympic glory.
- *Gymkata* long had a cult following, but for many years, it was difficult for fans to get their hands on a copy of this film. That changed in 2006, when *Gymkata* won an Amazon.com poll in which customers were asked what Warner Brothers film they'd like to see released on DVD. *Gymkata* won, making this classic available to a whole new generation of fans.

WHAT TO WATCH FOR

- Before reaching Parmistan, Cabot must first make a stopover in Karabal—a town that we're frequently reminded is "on the Caspian Sea." There's a little anti-American sentiment going around there, which leads to one of my favorite moments of the film. As a bonus, this also triggers the movie's first real fight scene.
- Over the course of the movie, you'll notice that Cabot's gymkata is aided greatly by the constant presence of objects that strongly resemble gymnastics equipment. Both a horizontal bar and a pommel horse make appearances in unlikely places.
- If you're looking for a job in Parmistan, I highly recommend applying for a position as a flag ninja. Your responsibilities will include holding flags and occasionally pointing with said flags. The benefits aren't great, but in this economy, what can you expect?
- *Gymkata's* most infamous scene takes place in the Village of the Crazies, a town that is apparently home to all of Parmistan's insane citizens. After a few run-ins with individual residents, Cabot then fights off an entire horde of villagers with the help of a well-placed pommel horse. Finally, he flees the scene in a slow-motion chase that might be terrifying if it weren't so ridiculous. By the time this scene is over, you won't be sure if you should laugh, cry, or watch it again in an attempt to figure out why anyone thought this sequence needed to be included.

BATTLEFIELD EARTH: A SAGA OF THE YEAR 3000
DIRECTED BY ROGER CHRISTIAN
WARNER BROTHERS, FRANCHISE PICTURES,
MORGAN CREEK PRODUCTIONS (2000)

There are bad movies, there are movies with big budgets, and there are movies that bomb at the box office. But if you want a movie that fits into all three of these categories simultaneously, you're looking at a much shorter list—one that *Battlefield Earth* is right at the top of. One of the most famous worst-movie-ever candidates, *Battlefield Earth* was plagued with issues from start to finish, and the result was a mess that was panned by viewers and critics alike.

The story of *Battlefield Earth* begins almost two decades before the release of the feature film. In 1982, Scientology founder L. Ron Hubbard wrote *Battlefield Earth: A Saga of the Year 3000*, a science-fiction novel over one thousand pages long. The book wasn't hailed as a classic by any means, and some critics did find it laughably bad, but others were more kind, and the novel has more than its fair share of fans to this day.

The book tells the tale of Jonnie Goodboy Tyler, a young man who lives on a future Earth that has been ruled by an alien race known as the Psychlos for about one thousand years. Jonnie is part of one of the few tribes of humans still living on the planet—situated near Denver. While exploring the ruins of the former city, Jonnie is captured by the Psychlo security chief, Terl.

As it happens, Terl isn't very happy about being assigned to Earth, where the Psychlos do little more than mine the planet for gold and other minerals. He's going to be stuck on the planet indefinitely, but he has a plan to go back as a very rich Psychlo: he has found a hidden stash of gold that the Psychlos can't get to—the gas they breathe explodes violently when combined with radioactive metals, and the gold deposits are located alongside uranium—and he plans on using human workers to mine it for him. Terl trains Jonnie and recruits other humans—known as "man animals" to the Psychlos—to do his bidding. Unbeknownst to him, though, the humans formulate a plot to kick the Psychlos off their planet once and for all.

A devoted Scientologist, John Travolta had long wanted to make a film adaptation that would follow the same plot as Hubbard's novel. But despite the fact that Travolta's name was attached to the project and that the book had a relatively solid fan base to draw on, it was surprisingly hard to find studios willing to work on the project. It seemed that the connection with Scientology was a problem, as studios were concerned that the controversy surrounding the religion might keep audiences away from theaters—though the script itself may have been enough to make major studios shy away regardless.

Eventually, Travolta struck a deal with Franchise Pictures, a short-lived independent production company responsible for well-received films like *The Boondock Saints* and *The Whole Nine Yards,* as well as flops like *Ballistic: Ecks vs. Sever.* Travolta himself stayed on with the project to play the role of Terl, while Barry Pepper played Jonnie and Forest Whitaker took the role of Ker, a Psychlo working with Ker.

Even before the film was released, the prospects for *Battlefield Earth* seemed shaky at best. Rumors floated about the terrible reactions from test audiences, and a leaked version of the screenplay—with an alternate title to disguise what was being read—received hilariously negative comments from Hollywood executives.

Then the movie was released and it only got worse.

To say that *Battlefield Earth* received poor reviews is a massive understatement. It's not that there aren't positive reviews of this movie out there, but finding one is like coming across a sacred white buffalo. Almost universally, *Battlefield Earth* was panned by critics—and they weren't calling it "mediocre" or "disappointing." Many people will point to its two percent score on Rotten Tomatoes to show how hated this film is, but that only shows that people didn't like it. If you want to understand the total hatred for the film, you need to take a look over at Metacritic, where professional reviewers have given the movie an average score in the single digits...out of a hundred.

What exactly did critics and viewers find so objectionable about *Battlefield Earth*? In short: everything. None of the performances in the film are great, but Travolta's is particularly worthy of ridicule, as he delivers lines in the most stilted manner possible. He doesn't just chew the scenery—he devours it whole. Even if the entire cast had given the performances of their lives, it wouldn't have rescued the screenplay, which was filled with numerous plot holes and unusual deviations from the source material—such as how exactly those fighter jets stayed in working condition for a millennium. The Psychlo costuming and makeup remains a source of easy jokes to this day—beyond simply looking ridiculous, there are inconsistencies throughout the film, such as the number of fingers on a Psychlo changing between five and six depending on which scene you're watching.

Many of the films in this book are failures in every regard, but none of them combine being quite this bad with having a massive budget to work with. That makes *Battlefield Earth* a textbook example of how not to make a blockbuster Hollywood film, as well as living proof that sometimes throwing money at a movie won't cover up all of its problems. It's also perfectly good fodder for your bad movie night, with plenty of memorable moments and quotable lines to dull the pain you'll endure for the two hours you devote to the film.

FUN FACTS

- *Battlefield Earth* actually only covers a little less than half of the novel it's based on. A sequel covering the second portion of the book—when Jonnie defends Earth against a number of potential conquerors—was slated to make up the plot of a sequel to the first film. Shockingly, that second film was never made.
- In what might be the movie's greatest success, *Battlefield Earth* won a total of nine Golden Raspberry Rewards. It initially won seven of the eight awards it was nominated

for in the 2001 Razzies, with only Forest Whitaker escaping victory for Worst Supporting Actor—the film even managed to win Worst Screen Couple, with the entry being "John Travolta and anyone sharing the screen with him". Later, *Battlefield Earth* would be honored by the Razzies in 2005 for the Worst Drama of Our First Twenty-Five Years, and again in 2010 as the Worst Picture of the Decade.

- *Battlefield Earth* would ultimately lead to the downfall of Franchise Pictures. However, it wasn't due to the box office failure. In fact, when you consider DVD sales and other revenue sources, it's even possible that the film might have made a few dollars. However, Franchise Pictures faced a lawsuit from investors who believed that the studio had committed fraud in claiming a budget of seventy-five million dollars. Later investigation led to the revelation that the actual budget for the movie turned out to be forty-four million. The final judgment allowed German investment group Intertainment AG to be awarded damages totaling more than one hundred and twenty-one million dollars—more than enough to put Franchise Pictures out of business.

WHAT TO WATCH FOR

- The amazing use of slow motion in this film. Well, it's much less amazing after the sixth or seventh time the action deliberately slows to a crawl.

- Did I mention that Travolta gets a little hammy in this movie? Because he was learning to ham it up while you were still learning how to spell your name!
- Here's a fun game to play: every time you notice an inconsistency in the plot, score a point. To avoid scores that rise into the hundreds, I suggest using a house rule that "item cannot still exist/be operational after one thousand years" is not a valid category for scoring purposes. Don't worry, basketball scores are still quite possible.
- At one point, Terl shoots the legs off of some cows to prove his proficiency as a marksman. No, this isn't supposed to be a comedy.
- The training sequence in which the humans—who are essentially as socially and mentally developed as cavemen—learn to pilot Harrier jets and prepare a nuclear warhead needs to be seen to be believed. Even if you can get by the improbability of the men getting up to speed on flying, that doesn't really explain why they're suddenly capable of communicating using twentieth century slang during a dogfight.

As Seen on MST3K

If there's an equivalent to the concept of a gateway drug in the bad movie world, it has to be Mystery Science Theater 3000. Like many others, I first learned all about the joy that could be found in watching the worst films imaginable with the help of a man stuck on a satellite with two wisecracking robots.

If you're not familiar with the show, Mystery Science Theater 3000—usually abbreviated as MST3K—was the creation of Joel Hodgson and began airing in 1988. It told the story of a man—first Hodgson playing a character named Joel Robinson, then later Michael J. Nelson playing the creatively named Mike Nelson—who was trapped by a mad scientist on the Satellite of Love. There, he had to endure watching an endless stream of bad movies as part of a psychological experiment. However, Joel made the process a little easier by building two robots—Tom Servo (voiced primarily by Kevin Murphy, and also by J. Elvis Weinstein) and Crow T. Robot (Trace Beaulieu, and later Bill Corbett)—who served to help mock the films they watched.

Each episode of MST3K was built around an *experiment*— one film that Joel or Mike would have to watch along with the robots. The film would be broken up by short host segments that took place outside of the theater, which often included sketches related to the film in question. But most of the show simply featured silhouettes of our heroes watching a movie from the front row of their theater, making jokes at the expense of the film at every opportunity.

In the introduction to the previous chapter, I talked about the kinds of films that served as good entry points into bad movie enjoyment. For many bad movie beginners, MST3K may actually be the perfect place to start—especially if you'd otherwise be braving these movies alone. One of the joys of watching a great bad movie is the ability to crack jokes with your friends while you watch. MST3K is an amazing introduction to this aspect of bad movie culture, as the movies come "pre-riffed" by the show. You can laugh along with the jokes while also coming up with your own, all of which serves as an introduction to how audience participation can make an otherwise terrible movie watchable and entertaining. Most of the MST3K cast has since moved on to other projects such as *RiffTrax*, which provides commentary tracks for a variety of more recent films (including several featured in this book).

In this chapter, you'll find a selection of movies that were featured on MST3K. It should go without saying that the episodes that feature these movies are worth watching, but that's not why I picked these particular films. Each of these choices can also be watched in its original form and still deliver plenty of laughs. True, some are definitely more painful without the help of the MST3K crew—I'm looking at you, *Manos*—but with

MANOS: THE HANDS OF FATE
DIRECTED BY HAROLD P. WARREN
NORM-IRIS, SUN CITY FILMS (1966)

A true contender in the race for the worst film ever made, *Manos: The Hands of Fate* has a backstory that's just as interesting as the movie itself. In fact, we're all very lucky—or unlucky, depending on your perspective—to have this movie around at all, as it easily could have been lost and forgotten about forever.

The story begins when director Harold Warren made a bet with a screenwriter friend. Convinced that making a horror movie was easy work, he wagered that he could make an entire film on his own. He raised money on his own, hired a cast and crew that agreed to work for a share of the profits rather than being paid up front, and began filming.

As it would turn out, filming was one of the biggest issues with the making of *Manos*. Not only did Warren use a camera that could only shoot about thirty-two seconds at a time, but the equipment was rented, meaning time was of the essence. Reshoots were almost unheard of, and technical limitations meant that all sound effects and dialogue had to be recorded after the fact, without much of the cast available to voice their parts.

Despite these issues, Warren succeeded in finishing his film and arranging for a premiere, which took place in his hometown of El Paso, Texas. Despite it being a gala event for the town, it quickly became apparent that the movie wasn't very good—we'll talk more about why in a moment. With even Warren realizing his movie was terrible, it's somewhat surprising to know that *Manos* did get a few screenings at a limited number of theaters in the area before seemingly falling off the face of the Earth.

Few things are forgotten forever, though, and the movie somehow managed to be distributed for home video—reportedly by suppliers specializing in public domain films. The movie would eventually be sent to the MST3K crew, who knew they had a movie that had to be seen by the masses.

Since then, *Manos* has become an indispensible part of bad movie culture. It's been referenced in television programs and video games, been adapted into a stage production, and there's even an effort underway to restore the film so that it can be re-released in high definition. Anytime someone makes a list of the worst films ever, you can rest assured that *Manos* will appear at or near the top. So, what makes this movie so notoriously awful?

Manos begins as a story about a family road trip. After several scintillating minutes in which a car travels along some unremarkable country roads, we meet Michael (played by Warren himself), his wife Margaret (Diane Mahree), and their daughter, Debbie (Jackey Neyman), who are traveling along with their dog to a vacation resort known as Valley Lodge. They aren't too successful in their search, instead coming across a house that's tended by Torgo (John Reynolds).

Torgo is the true star of *Manos*. Presumably, he was meant to be a satyr, though this is never actually referenced in the film. Torgo walks slowly and with a strange gait, thanks to wearing coat hangers under his pants—but this effect is somewhat mitigated by the fact that his feet are rarely visible, and even when they are, it's often unclear whether he's wearing his prosthetic hooves. Still, Torgo is strange, and he claims that he's only taking care of the house while "the Master" is away.

Told that there is no way out before night falls, the family prepares to spend the night at the house. They soon deal with a strange series of events, including Torgo declaring his lust for Margaret, the family dog dying mysteriously, and a whole lot of creepy talk about the Master.

Soon enough, the Master (Tom Neyman) makes his appearance, as do his lovely wives. It seems that Margaret and Debbie might both be future Mrs. Masters, though not all of the current wives agree with this fate. This eventually leads to one of the most famous scenes in the film—an all-out brawl between the Master's wives that serves very little purpose, but certainly livens up the film for a few minutes.

From there, the film heads inevitably toward a predictable conclusion. The family eventually comes face-to-face with the Master, and must attempt to defend themselves or escape before becoming trapped in the house forever. Also, some bad stuff might happen to Torgo, which is sad, because Torgo is by far the best thing *Manos* has going for it. I won't spoil the ending, though you might wish I had: now you'll need to actually watch all seventy-four minutes of the movie in order to find out what happens.

There's so much going on with this movie that it's hard to know what to share with you and what to leave for you to discover on your own. There's a recurring subplot with a young couple making out in a car and being told to move along by police officers that was only added in after the actress in these scenes hurt her leg, and was no longer able to serve as one of the Master's wives. There's the fact that in many instances, the sound track of the film doesn't stay in sync with the action on the screen. And then there's the editing, which—while certainly not helped by the previously mentioned limitations of the camera being used—is so bizarre that it needs to be seen to be believed.

With some of the worst pacing around and hilariously bad acting and writing, *Manos: The Hands of Fate* is certain to remain one of the true masterpieces of bad cinema. Every bad movie fan owes a debt of gratitude to all those that have helped—and continue to help—keep Manos from disappearing from the world in the way that so many older films and television shows have. While it might truly be one of the worst movies ever made, it's also one that every bad movie fan needs to see at least once.

FUN FACTS

- The working title for this film was The Lodge of Sins. After the name changed in post-production, the remaining crew preferred to refer to the clearly underwhelming film as Mangos: The Cans of Fruit.

- Convinced that he had created the worst film ever, Warren thought his film might make a decent comedy— if it were to be redubbed in the mode of *What's Up, Tiger Lily?*, the 1966 Woody Allen movie that took a Japanese filmed and dubbed over the original dialogue. Warren's idea was never put into practice.

NOT-SO-FUN FACT

One of the saddest things about the making of *Manos: The Hands of Fate* was that one of its stars wasn't able to attend the film's premiere, and would never know it became a cult classic. John Reynolds—the man who played Torgo—committed suicide just a month before the movie was set to premiere. While some sources claim that Reynolds damaged his knees while wearing Torgo's leg prosthetics during filming, it's unclear whether the suicide had anything to do with the making of the film.

SPACE MUTINY
DIRECTED BY DAVID WINTERS AND NEAL SUNDSTROM
A.I.P. PRODUCTIONS (1988)

Imagine a movie about a spaceship that has been traveling through space for generations. Some aboard the ship are unhappy about never having actually lived on a planet and decide to stage a mutiny. It's a pretty simple concept and there are dozens of directions you could go in order to create drama, suspense, and action.

Now, try imagining the worst possible movie you could envision based around this concept, and you have some idea of what *Space Mutiny* is all about.

The story begins aboard the Southern Sun, a large spaceship that is carrying tens of thousands of people in search of a planet to colonize. This isn't something that Flight Commander Elijah Kalgan (John Phillip Law) can deal with, so he plots with space pirates to hijack the Southern Sun and direct it toward a star system where he can presumably force the ship to land on a planet.

Opposing the mutineers is Dave Ryder (Reb Brown), who helps Commander Alex Jansen (Cameron Mitchell) save his ship while also falling in love with Jansen's daughter, Dr. Lea Jansen (Cisse Cameron). Ryder rallies the troops and manages to defeat Kalgan, allowing the passengers of the Southern Stars to continue drifting aimlessly through the stars.

The plot is nothing spectacular, but it's not embarrassing. No, where Space Mutiny earns its place among the worst films ever made is in its production, which is downright laughable. Here's a quick list of a few of the major issues you'll notice during your first viewing:

- All of the exterior space shots in the film are created using stock footage from the original *Battlestar Galactica* television series.

- The interior of the ship features some interesting design choices. For instance, the ship appears to have a basement complete with brick walls and windows that are letting in plenty of sunlight.
- There are several dramatic chase scenes that have characters fighting while driving Enforcers, which appear to be modified golf carts or floor-buffers.
- At one point, a character dies, only to later appear back at her desk working in a later scene. Apparently, continuity wasn't at a premium here.

That's just a small sampling of the fun you can expect watching *Space Mutiny*. Reb Brown turns in a vintage performance, throwing in plenty of grunts and yells at every opportunity. You'll also learn lots about the future by spending time in the on-board dance club and marveling at the wall-mounted keyboards found throughout the ship. You'll meet the Bellerians—a group of women who barely factor into the plot at all. And you'll wonder why the captain and his daughter appear to be approximately the same age.

I would be remiss if I didn't point out that the creation of *Space Mutiny* had at least one positive real world consequence. Reb Brown and Cisse Cameron were introduced to each other on this film and would eventually fall in love. The two were later married and remain together to this day.

In all other aspects, however, *Space Mutiny* is a film that only a fan of the worst in cinema could love. It is probably one of the worst science fiction movies ever created, and is one of the few films featured on MST3K that is just as much fun to watch and riff on its own.

Edward Scimia

HOBGOBLINS
DIRECTED BY RICK SLOANE
RICK SLOANE PRODUCTIONS (1988)

It's not easy deciding where to start when discussing *Hobgoblins*. This movie is one part horror, one part comedy, and two parts *Gremlins* rip-off. Most importantly, it's entirely terrible. Also, there's a rake fight. We'll get back to that in a bit.

Like most people, I first saw *Hobgoblins* on MST3K, though I've since been unfortunate enough to also watch the film in its original state. There are certainly films in which the addition of a couple scenes that were cut out of the MST3K version make the movie a bit better or more comprehensible. Rest assured that *Hobgoblins* is not one of those films.

The movie is about a group of young adult friends, with the focus being squarely on Kevin (Tom Barlett), who has recently started a job as a security guard at an abandoned film studio. He's dating Amy (Paige Sullivan), a quiet and reserved woman who wishes that Kevin would accomplish more with his life. Daphne (Kelley Palmer) is a sex-obsessed party girl who is excited about the return of her boyfriend Nick (Billy Frank), who is serving in the Army. The group is rounded out by Kyle (Steven Boggs), who is a nerd because...every movie group needs a nerd.

Kevin is warned by senior security guard Mr. McCreedy (Jeffrey Culver) that he should never open a particular vault on the studio lot. Shockingly, Kevin quickly finds himself in that vault and unleashes the titular hobgoblins upon the world. McCreedy tells him that the hobgoblins crashed in a spaceship many years ago, and that he had stayed at the studio in order to ensure that they would never get out.

The hobgoblins have a power that, in a better movie, could have been quite interesting. It seems that they can make the people around them experience their deepest fantasies, but that this comes at a price, as most people inevitably end up dead as a result. The bookish Amy, for instance, ends up performing at a sleazy club, while another fantasy has Kevin showing his bravery to Amy. Kyle has a fantasy that leads to him making out with a phone sex operator, while Nick sees himself in charge of an attack on the hobgoblins.

Does this sound reasonable so far? Let's absolve you of any notions about the quality of this film. Let's list a few of the more infamous moments from *Hobgoblins* so that you can judge for yourself:

- The rake fight scene: if you're not sure if you want to watch this movie or not, you merely need look online for a video of the rake fight. You will find about two minutes of the most intense garden equipment fighting ever caught on film, as Nick shows Kevin his expertise in hoe-to-hoe combat.
- Kyle's subplot is all about calling a 1-800 sex line. At one point, we see a phone sex operator issuing some standard issue dirty talk, only with a very unusual twist:

she appears to be having the conversation with herself, delivering half her lines with an imitation male voice.

- The entire Club Scum sequence—and not just because of the venue's great name. Most everything about the club is absurd, but the band that plays when they first arrive takes the cake. As pointed out in the MST3K episode devoted to *Hobgoblins,* it's hard to figure out exactly what the band is singing about, though Mike and the robots make a few good guesses, like "Pig Licker" and "Fish Picker." For the record, they're actually saying "Kiss Kicker," though it's hard to imagine anyone figuring that out unless they knew the title of the song.

- The hobgoblins themselves are hilarious. I mean, it's clear they were designed to be scary, but they're also strangely adorable. You might feel the urge to reach out and pet one.

-

I don't know what else to say about this movie other than to give *Hobgoblins* the highest recommendation to bad movie fans. Even director Rick Sloane knew he had something special on his hands, as he submitted the film to MST3K himself knowing they would skewer it mercilessly. On the other hand, the 2009 sequel, *Hobgoblins 2,* might be just a little too self-aware for some, as it was designed to look and feel as much like the original as possible, down to the 80s clothing and plenty of jokes that come at the expense of the first film.

WEREWOLF
DIRECTED BY TONY ZARINDAST
TOZART PUBLISHING INC. (1996)

Werewolves are in vogue these days, usually as an alternative love interest in vampire-based stories. Until recently, though, werewolves were deadly monsters instead of cuddly protectors. The direct-to-VHS film *Werewolf* was designed to showcase the more horrific variety of lycanthrope—a creature that hunted by the full moon and spread its curse by biting victims.

In *Werewolf*, the story starts with an archaeological dig in Arizona. Workers there dig up what appears to be a werewolf skeleton, and when foreman Yuri (Jorge Rivero) starts a fight, digger Tommy (Jules Desjarlais) is scratched by the skeleton. Lead archaeologist Noel (Richard Lynch) outlines what he knows of werewolf legend, and before long, Tommy is in a hospital and turning into a werewolf.

The movie then takes us to a party, where another archaeologist, Natalie (Adrianna Miles), is introduced to Paul (Fedrico Cavalli), a writer. They hit it off, making Yuri jealous enough to create a new werewolf by injecting Tommy's blood into a security guard at his research lab. This is the impetus for the first great scene in *Werewolf*, as the security guard drives home, changes into his wolf form, and then crashes his car into a pile of barrels that have decided to take up residence in the middle of a busy road. The car in turn explodes, killing the werewolf.

Paul visits the lab with Natalie the next day, and once again, Yuri starts a fight. This results in Paul being wounded by the werewolf skeleton, which naturally means it is his turn to be-come a werewolf. Through the rest of the film, Paul kills at night while Natalie and Yuri try to track him down.

It's a fairly standard horror movie plot to be sure, but as usual, the devil is in the details. Adrianna Miles is certainly an attrac-tive actress, but her command of the English language left some-thing to be desired in this film. She has trouble pronouncing the word "werewolf," with it usually coming out something more like "wurwilf." Some of her other line reads are questionable as well, such as her impassioned plea to Yuri: "You and Noel is in it for fame and fortune? But over my dead body!"

Other characters have their moments as well. Sam (R.C. Bates)—the Keeper of the home that Paul is staying in—is a truly bizarre character who makes pronouncements about Dracula's sexual preferences and showing an interesting mix of fear and bravery in the face of a werewolf attack. Budget movie veteran Joe Estevez even makes an appearance as Joel, one of the workers at the archeological site.

Without ruining the entire movie, there are a few other scenes that require mentioning. It seems they don't make werewolves like they used to and we're treated to a couple examples of their futility. We're told to fear werewolves—though they apparently struggle mightily to defeat random bystanders in fistfights and need their victims to slow down and fall a few times in order to catch them. Perhaps the varying abilities of the werewolves has something to do with their changing appearance—sometimes they look like wolves, other times more like bears, and occasion-ally like men with a small amount of makeup on.

With endless material to riff, it's no surprise that *Werewolf* remains one of the most popular MST3K episodes ever filmed. If you try watching it on its own, you'll get plenty of enjoyment out of it—though I'd still recommend giving the MST3K version a watch if you haven't yet, if only to take part in the classic sing-along performed by Mike and the bots over the credits.

THE FINAL SACRIFICE
DIRECTED BY TJARDUS GREIDANUS
FLYING DUTCHMAN PRODUCTIONS LTD.
(1990)

In my personal circle of MST3K fans, there may be no character from any of the movies featured on the show more beloved than Zap Rowsdower (Bruce J. Mitchell), the hero of *Final Sacrifice*. Rowsdower is an unlikely hero, but his antics in *Final Sacrifice* have made him a living legend— once you've watched this film, you'll understand why.

The Final Sacrifice—better known simply as *Final Sacrifice*, and less well known under the alternate title *Quest for the Lost City*—begins with a teenage boy named Troy McGreggor (Christian Malcolm) finding a mysterious map that had be-longed to his late father. Troy wants to find out what really happened to his dad, so he starts trying to contact people who are mentioned in and around the map and other documents his father left behind. This attracts the attention of a deadly cult, which makes several attempts to kill Troy. He runs, and eventually runs into Rowsdower—a drifter who initially wants nothing to do with Troy.

Slowly, Troy and Rowsdower begin to bond. The two travel through the Alberta wilderness, eventually coming across Mike Pipper (Ron Anderson), a former partner of Troy's father. Pipper is grizzled—to say the least—and his line delivery is one of the great highlights of *Final Sacrifice*. He tells Troy about an ancient civilization known as the Ziox, one that was extremely advanced, but was all-but destroyed after they turned away from their god. The cult is made up of the remaining remnants of the Ziox, led by Satoris, a man who believes he can bring the Ziox back to their former glory. The rest of the film sees Rowsdower and Troy attempting to stop the cult from reviving the lost city of the Ziox.

It's a weak premise, but on its own, it wouldn't be a particularly noteworthy for a low-budget film. What really makes *Final Sacrifice* so memorable is Rowsdower himself, a man who is one of the least inspiring heroes in the history of film. Rowsdower is a surly, overweight Canadian man who drinks heavily and has a severe case of hockey hair. Somehow, this combination makes him unforgettable and loveable, even while he treats Troy with distain and only reluctantly joins the quest to save the world.

Granted, that's not the only reason you'll want to give *Final Sacrifice* a look. Troy is hilariously irritating—particularly each time he says "Rowsdower!"—and is best remembered for his red sweater, rather than anything he accomplishes during the movie.

As mentioned earlier, Pipper is also a gift that keeps on giving—he'll likely remind you more of a nineteenth century gold prospector than a man who can help bring down an ancient and powerful cult. And if all else fails, you can always have fun saying Ziox over and over again. It's pronounced *zee-ox!*

Final Sacrifice is one of the most popular MST3K episodes of all, and for good reason. While it's a movie that certainly remains fun in its original form, you and your friends will have a tough time topping the riffs made by Mike and the bots in this one. If you've never seen this episode, it's one you need to watch—either before or after braving *Final Sacrifice* in its original form.

MERLIN'S SHOP OF MYSTICAL WONDERS
DIRECTED BY KENNETH J. BERTON
MONARCH VIDEO (1996)

While some consider it to be frighteningly terrible—it has a solid place on the IMDB Bottom 100 list—*Merlin's Shop of Mystical Wonders* has a special place in my heart, and remains to this day one of my personal favorite MST3K episodes. It tells the story of Merlin, the most famous wizard of all time, and the misadventures he finds himself in when he opens a store in modern times. It's a goofy premise, but what's wrong with that?

Okay, this film does have a few issues. Perhaps the biggest is the fact that it's not really a single story—it's two separate films stitched together and connected through a few cutaways to Ernest Borgnine telling a bedtime story to his grandson. Neither of these stories is particularly interesting, and mashing them together...well, let's just say that the transition isn't exactly seamless.

The movie begins with a young boy watching a horror film on television. When the power goes out, the boy's grandfather, Borgnine, tells him a story about Merlin to keep him occupied. The story involves a married couple, Madeline (Patricia Sansone) and Jonathan (John Terrence) who are having difficulty conceiving a child. Madeline is very concerned about this, while Jonathan is consumed with his work as a newspaper columnist, where he reviews just about anything, apparently. Walking into Merlin's shop, Jonathan mocks the entire premise of the store, doubting that Merlin is who he says he is. Merlin decides to prove himself by giving his spell book to Jonathan, who is disbelieving—until he goes home and tries some of the spells on his own.

When that story ends, the child still isn't ready for bed, so grandpa tells another story. This one barely features Merlin at all, and instead ties up a loose end from the first part of the film when a thief stole a toy monkey from the shop. While there are a few scenes showing Merlin trying to track down the monkey, the main plot is about the family who ended up in possession of the toy, and their battle with the evil spirit that inhabits it. In reality, this part of the film is actually repurposed footage from a film known as *The Devil's Gift*, which features an entirely different cast, filming style, and tone than the material created specifically for *Merlin's Shop*. It's also the segment that contains many of the most memorable moments of the film, including the famous rock 'n' roll Martian song.

Beyond the obviously pieced-together nature of the film, that tone issue is probably the most striking problem with this movie. Given the framing device of a grandfather telling a story to a young boy and the whimsical nature of Merlin throughout the film, it's clear that the movie was designed to appeal to children. But there are a few instances during each portion of the movie that probably won't seem too charming to the young ones. For instance:

- Jonathan makes his pet cat demonic, and then defends himself by breathing fire, burning the cat alive.
- A demon accosts Jonathan through his mirror, warning him of the consequences of performing magic.
- In the second half of the movie, the evil monkey toy is responsible for the death of the family dog.
- Later, the father (David, played by Bob Mendelsohn) is nearly thrown into a gorge that opens up beneath him and then has a tree fall on top of him as the monkey attempts to kill him.
- Finally, the monkey locks the entire family inside of their house and is ready to kill them all before Merlin steps in at the last second to save the day. This is a departure from *The Devil's Gift*, in which the family is ultimately killed. This would have worked to soften the film, if it weren't for the fact that you can still hear the screams of the dying family in the background of the edited version.

Given the absurdity of trying to piece together the two films into something coherent, and the fact that it's by no means boring, *Merlin's Shop of Mystical Wonders* is definitely watchable either with or without the help of the MST3K commentary. I've also seen *The Devil's Gift* in its original form, which is almost two hours long—far longer than the entirety of *Merlin's Shop*, which shows just how much they cut out in order to try to make it into a family-friendly portion of the Merlin story. It's entertainingly bad as well, but I'd recommend seeing it only after you've experienced the much more ridiculous *Merlin's Shop* first.

Martial Arts Movies

For as long as I can remember, B-movies and the martial arts have been joined at the hip. Perhaps it's because you can put on a good show with a talented martial artist even without a great script, convincing special effects, or great actors. All of these expenses can be safely left out if you have a charismatic star who can beat up villains for ninety minutes.

That's not to suggest that all, or even most, martial arts flicks are bad movies. For instance, it's easy to look at a badly dubbed—or incompetently subtitled—film from Asia and laugh at it, especially if it was made on a low budget. But not being an expert on martial arts myself, it's hard for me to pick these movies apart. Who am I to say if the man who just knocked down a dozen ninjas isn't putting on a good show for the audience? If I understood the language and the culture these movies were made in, isn't it possible that I'd realize that they're good or even great films?

This still leaves plenty of films in this genre that are undoubtedly so bad they're good. I've already covered one such film in *Gymkata*, and it's far from the only martial arts movie worthy of inclusion—there are yet more picks in later chapters that offer additional bad movie recommendations. The movies in this chapter aren't all strictly based around fast kicks and flurries of punches, but all of them have a strong martial arts theme, and they're all gloriously bad. They feature rapping kung fu masters, scheming billionaires that take revenge through karate, and evil ninjas that possess young ladies. Most importantly, they're all a blast to watch.

CITY DRAGON
DIRECTED BY "PHILTHY" PHIL PHILLIPS
LISA-FILM, PEACOCK FILMS, SMOOTH
SAILING PRODUCTIONS (1995)

Sometimes, it's clear that a movie was designed to vault some-one involved in the production into stardom. In the case of *City Dragon,* there were two men who seemingly thought this film would launch their careers: Stan Derain and Phil Phillips.

Derain—credited as MC Kung Fu—is the star of the film, play-ing the main character Ray. As you might be able to guess from Derain's stage name, Ray is something of a renaissance man. He's a martial artist, a rapper, and a world-class womanizer. Meanwhile, Phillips plays a character named Philthy, one of Ray's sidekicks who pals around with him while he picks up chicks. Along with starring in the film, Derain and Phillips also shared the writing credits, with Phillips also directing. They also combined to create the film's soundtrack, which features such hits as "Night Swim" and "Chemistry."

The movie follows Ray around as he hooks up with a couple of different women, occasionally gets into fights, and speaks in rhymes. There are some occasional musical interludes as well, including one that's hastily edited in after a sex scene. Lovely! Ray is joined on this adventure by his friends, Philthy and Rick (John Williams), who combine to make one heck of a trio.

After the hooking-up-with-girls portion of the film, we're introduced to Tina (Kathy Barbour), the woman who will make Ray end his player ways and finally settle down with her. Matters are complicated by Tina's abusive ex-boyfriend, John (John J. Haran), who spends much of the film in a mental institution while Tina is pregnant with his baby. Still, true love cannot be denied, and Tina and Ray are ultimately married.

Sadly, the marriage is a rough one. It seems that rhyming and martial arts don't pay enough to support a family, so Ray has to find a job. He proves quite capable of doing...whatever it is he does at his new job, but finds himself in the all-too-common situation of having a boss who wants him to sleep with her. Threatened with losing his job, he relents, but is eventually found out by Tina, nearly ruining their relationship.

The finale to the film has Tina give birth to her baby, while John escapes from the mental hospital. Ray and John have one final fight on a rooftop over the baby before Ray and Tina walk off happily into the sunset.

City Dragon offers viewers a unique blend of bad movie delights. The plot makes little sense, the dialogue is hilarious, and the songs performed by the stars are memorable—though probably not for the reasons they were shooting for. The fight scenes are also ridiculous, and only become more entertainingly silly as the movie goes on.

As for the film being the vehicle to turn MC Kung Fu and "Philthy" Phil Phillips into stars, it didn't quite get them there. *City Dragon* is the only movie they ever worked on.

WHAT TO WATCH FOR

- In the early portion of the movie, Ray spends most of his time sleeping with as many women as possible, but he's not a total jerk. We see him leave a note for one of his flings after he leaves. It even rhymes! Classy.
- As if to give you a reminder of what you could be watching, one scene that takes place in a video rental store—remember those?—features a number of better movies on the shelves, including *Star Wars*.
- Later on, Ray is forced into a fight at his dojo when a group of men come in and insult Bruce Lee. This personally offends Ray, who defeats his opponents in Lee's name. He then dedicates his victory to his martial arts hero, which triggers a poorly conceived musical cue.
- In the climactic fight scene, Ray and John get into a rather heated fight on a hospital roof. This would be fine and all, except that they're fighting in the same area where they laid a baby on the ground—you know, where you put a newborn when you want to keep it safe. This oversight

might be explained by the fact that they clearly used a doll in everything but the extreme close-up shots, which makes it a little less disturbing when Ray appears to accidentally hit the doll during the fight.

THE KARATE KID, PART III
DIRECTED BY JOHN G. AVILDSEN
COLUMBIA PICTURES (1989)

The Karate Kid is one of the quintessential movies of the 1980s. It told the story of Daniel LaRusso (Ralph Macchio), a high school student who learns karate from the wise Mr. Miyagi (Pat Morita). Daniel learns some lessons, defeats more or less the entire Cobra Kai dojo in a tournament, and even wins the affections of a young Elisabeth Shue. It's a cheesy film, but not a terrible one. This was followed up by *The Karate Kid, Part II*—a rather underwhelming sequel that sends Daniel and Miyagi on an adventure to Japan that involves storms, little hand drums, and honking their opponents' noses.

Which brings us to the movie we're most interested in: *The Karate Kid, Part III*. The third installment of the series is supposed to take place about a year after the first film, pretty much picking up immediately after Daniel and Miyagi return from Japan. John Kreese (Martin Kove), the sensei at the Cobra Kai dojo, finds himself on hard times. All of his students have abandoned him after his behavior at last year's karate tournament, and he's ready to give up on the business. Before he packs it in, though, he visits his old war buddy, Terry Silver (Thomas Ian Griffith), who is now an extraordinarily wealthy businessman. Silver sends Kreese to Tahiti on a vacation, promising to get revenge on Daniel and Mr. Miyagi for ruining his life.

Oh, and what a revenge it will be. Silver comes up with an impressively circuitous plan to take revenge on Daniel, one that requires him to hire outsider Mike Barnes (Sean Kanan)—known as "Karate's Bad Boy"—to move to the valley and compete in next year's tournament specifically to beat the crap out of Daniel. In the meantime, he takes a number of contrived steps to make Daniel forget everything that Mr. Miyagi taught him over the last two movies.

Let's think about that for a minute. Here you have a multimillionaire, perhaps even a billionaire, who is taking many months out of his life to ruin the lives of an eighteen-year-old kid and an old Japanese man. Do we really need to go into why this is hilarious? We don't see Bill Gates going around interfering in Little League baseball games. Then again, that would probably be incredibly entertaining—and so is this film.

Sure enough, it's Silver who steals the show. From the first scenes of the movie, Griffith gives an incredibly hammy performance as the movie's villain. You'll know he's the villain right off the bat, as just about the first thing we hear him talking about is finding ways to discretely dump toxic waste in foreign countries. Never before has a villain been so enthusiastic about the ruination of an inconsequential teenage boy. Did I mention the name of his company is Dynatox Industries? Yes, he's evil.

If you're worried that this movie might be filled with too much boring action, you're in for a pleasant surprise. *Part III* is filled with everything fans of this series were clamoring for—a look at the difficulties of opening a bonsai tree shop, plenty of contract negotiations, and lots of Daniel endlessly jabbering on every time he delivers a line in what must have been an attempt at ad-libbing gone horribly wrong.

The movie plays out as you would expect: Daniel must defend his title at the All-Valley Karate Tournament. Daniel is aided by a very convenient rule that only requires him to fight in the championship round, where he faces off against Barnes. The final fight would normally stick out as being particularly absurd, but in a movie like this one, you'll barely even care.

The Karate Kid: Part III is easily the worst film in the series, but there's no denying that it's incredibly entertaining. In the words of Terry Silver, this movie is *perfect* for any bad movie night.

WHAT TO WATCH FOR

- Ralph Macchio was already in his twenties when he filmed *The Karate Kid*, but he was still passable as the teenaged Daniel in that movie. This time around, Macchio was twenty-seven and had noticeably put on some weight, both of which stretched the believability of him playing an eighteen-year-old karate champion.

- I mentioned above that Terry Silver stole the show, but there's another member of Team Dynatox who's also worth keeping an eye on. One of Silver's young henchmen is named Snake, and he's often seen hanging around with Mike Barnes as they terrorize Daniel through much of the film. Any scene with Snake brings a little something extra to the table, as he tends to be nearly as flamboyantly evil as Silver himself.

- That said, you can't beat the performance of Thomas Ian Griffith as Terry Silver. Seriously, it's a thing of brilliance. Griffith must have known that the role was ridiculous to begin with, so he plays it up as much as humanly possible. The laugh, the smile, the way every line reminds us that he's pure evil—it all comes together to make him one of the most memorable bad movie villains around.

POCKET NINJAS

DIRECTED BY DONALD G. JACKSON, DAVID HUEY, AND DAVE EDDY

CINE EXCEL ENTERTAINMENT (1994)

If you've ever had one of those fever dreams where completely disparate elements and settings flow together on a surreal landscape, you'll have some understanding of what to expect from *Pocket Ninjas*. Be warned, though: there's a good chance that your dream made much more sense. Trying to write a plot summary for this film is an exercise in futility, as it's unclear whether or not there is any coherent plot that binds the entire film together. There are a few ninjas, maybe, and the main characters more of less remain the same throughout the movie. Other than that, you're on your own.

Okay, let's try backing up a bit to make some sense of this mess. In 1991, Donald G. Jackson directed and produced *The Roller Blade Seven*, a film that showcased a style that Jackson and co-producer—and star—Scott Shaw called "Zen filmmaking." The idea was to create a film with only a loose idea of what would occur, with no script and minimal direction. Essentially, the filmmakers would just film the movie without any expectations, worrying about how to tie all their footage together later on. This produced some *interesting* results.

Three years later, producer David Huey found himself wishing to make a movie out of a script written by Mark Williams, then titled *Skate Dragons*. He brought in Jackson to direct, thinking that with the Zen filmmaking style and the Williams script, he might be able to create a children's version of *The Roller Blade Seven*.

Unfortunately, Huey wasn't pleased with the early results, and removed Jackson from the film. Huey took over and completed the film on his own, writing a few new scenes to go along with the original Williams screenplay. He then brought in Dave Eddy to figure out a way to tie the entire film together, which required further additions to the script. Finally, what we now know as *Pocket Ninjas* was complete.

With a creative process like that, you might expect *Pocket Ninjas* to be a little bit disjointed, but you'd never expect a film quite like what was released. The film ostensibly follows the adventures of three young martial arts heroes: Steve (Brad Bufanda), Damien (Joseph Valencia), and Tanya (credited only as "Sondi"). They are taught by their master, an Australian man known as the White Dragon (Gary Daniels). Over the course of the film, the three teenagers battle a gang called the Stingers, nominally led by Cobra Khan (Robert Z'Dar).

The way this conflict plays out on screen is unusual. Sometimes, battles take place on roller skates, while at other times, they take place in a balloon factory. Parts of the movie seem like they were designed to be taken seriously, while other scenes feature corny jokes and comical sound effects. There are several martial arts training montages, some of which feature people who are most certainly not martial artists.

The whole movie is tied together by scenes that take place in a tree house—Eddy's contribution—in which the three children read a Japanese comic book about the White Dragon. They take turns imagining what the comic might actually say, with their imagined scenarios playing out on screen. It might have sounded like a clever way to cobble together some unrelated footage, but it actually manages to make matters even more confusing. What's real? What's from the comic? Does the White Dragon even exist? Your guess is as good as mine.

There's no sugarcoating it: this movie is painful and it's probably downright unwatchable if you attempt to get through it alone. Even with friends, you will spend the entire eighty minutes (oh, it feels so much longer than that) wondering why anyone thought this movie should be made and why you're subjecting yourself to such torture. But if you remember to laugh at the absurdity of it all, crack a few jokes, and console each other when it feels like you can't go on, you might just join the ranks of the brave few who have survived an entire viewing of Pocket Ninjas.

WHAT TO WATCH FOR

- There are some strange voiceovers placed throughout the film. They're presumably being spoken in the future by one of the main characters, who is fondly looking back on his childhood. Like everything else in this film, they rarely make any sense.
- About halfway through the film, Damien's mother shows up as a potential love interest for the White Dragon. They hit it off, only for this plot point never to be mentioned again. Later, the mother is kidnapped after she chases a coupon being pulled down a sidewalk by a wire. Yes, that really happens.
- The "Sonic Virtual Reality" scene near the end of the film is truly breathtaking. This sequence is bizarre, even by the lofty standards of Pocket Ninjas, with the characters fighting each other in what appears to be an immersive 3D fighting video game. Of course, none of this has any bearing on the rest of the film whatsoever and does nothing to resolve any of the outstanding issues with the plot.

Edward Scimia

NINJA 3: THE DOMINATION DIRECTED BY SAM FIRSTENBERG CANNON FILMS, GOLAN–GLOBUS PRODUCTIONS (1984)

Whatever else I might say about *Ninja 3: The Domination*, there's one positive for this movie: you don't have to have seen the first two Ninja films (*Enter the Ninja* and *Revenge of the Ninja*) in order to understand what's going on in this film. The movies have absolutely nothing to do with one another, so you can start right with *The Domination* and not feel like you're missing anything.

This is a good thing, because you'll have enough to deal with in this film alone. *Ninja 3* begins with a ninja (David Chung) fighting a rampaging mob of golf course attendants, along with a few golfers. In the first few minutes of the film, you'll see this ninja stop a moving golf cart by grabbing it with one hand, kill a police officer by stabbing his sword through the roof of a car, take down a police helicopter by leaping onto it from a tree, and sink a chip shot from the bunker on the sixteenth hole. All right, that last one didn't happen, but keep in mind that it was easily the least ridiculous thing described in this paragraph, and it's the only one I made up.

Still, this unstoppable ninja menace does eventually meet his match. Oh sure, this only happens when he's surrounded by dozens of police officers, most of whom he manages to kill before finally being taken down in a hail of bullets. And he manages to fake his death before actually going down and then gets shot a few hundred more times. Then it turns out he was hiding and manages to crawl away when the cops aren't looking. Ninjas are made of magic!

Believe it or not, the plot of this movie hasn't even really started yet. Still not dead, the ninja scampers away to die near a woman named Christie (Lucinda Dickey), who is working to repair a nearby telephone line. Near death, the ninja struggles with Christie before finally transferring his spirit to her.

Christie starts acting a little differently now that she's possessed by a magic ninja spirit. She's strong enough to beat up gangs of men who are trying to harass her and occasionally kills one of the few cops who survived the initial ninja onslaught. There's also an arcade machine cabinet in her rather oddly furnished apartment—for reasons that are never explained. She's sometimes able to hold off the spirit by doing aerobics or dancing to 80s music, but that only works for so long.

Eventually, her boyfriend Billy (Jordan Bennett)—who is also a cop—decides that maybe things here aren't entirely on the level. He takes Christie to a Japanese spiritualist who hangs her by chains in the middle of a room. Christie never questions why this is necessary or how this might help remove her inner ninja, but it still doesn't help: the ninja exorcism fails, resulting in Christie's body flipping over a few times.

Christie and Billy learn the awful truth: that only a ninja can destroy a ninja. Luckily enough, a ninja named Yamada (Sho

Kosugi) shows up at this point in order to get his revenge against the evil ninja that has now taken residence inside Christie. This leads to a duel between Yamada and Ninja Christie, which ultimately leads to the movie's final conflict: can Yamada get rid of the evil ninja spirit without killing our heroine? We eventually get the answer, but not before Yamada gets to battle some warrior monks who are brainwashed by the evil ninja. Yeah, you read that right.

Ninja 3: The Domination is a thoroughly entertaining movie. The plot is thin enough to make it almost non-existent, but after watching the first rampaging ninja scene, you're not going to care one bit about the story. This movie is all about ridiculous ninja antics, with a splash in 1980s cheese thrown in for good measure. Add in the fact that Sho Kosugi's martial arts scenes are very impressive—he's pretty much the king of the 1980s ninja movie—and you have a film that delivers an enjoyably terrible ninety minutes of ninja action.

Sports Movies

I once had a professor who told me that both the best and the worst writing at any given newspaper could often be found in the sports section. That might well be a reflection of the fact that sports bring out the best and the worst in all of us. Sports can teach us about fair play, build communities, and lead to moments of brilliance, but they can also lead to ugly incidents, horrific injuries, and a dangerous mentality that turns fans of opposing teams into warring tribes.

Sports movies can be this way, too. There are examples of movies about sports that rank among the finest films ever created: *Rocky, Field of Dreams, Hoosiers* and others are favorites of critics and fans alike. But there are so many other terrible sports movies out there—and I couldn't possibly write this book without including at least a few of them.

One of the great things about sports films is that there's usually something to keep us interested in the movie, or at least something we can have fun analyzing to death while we're waiting for the movie to end. Take the following example:

TEEN WOLF
DIRECTED BY ROD DANIEL
WOLFKILL (1985)

This movie is a silly Michael J. Fox vehicle in which Fox plays Scott Howard, a high school student who is decidedly mediocre at basketball—and in most other aspects of his life. One day, Scott realizes that he's no ordinary human: he comes from a long line of werewolves. Being a werewolf is awkward, but it also comes with some benefits—chiefly, it apparently makes you really good at basketball. He learns this when he transforms into his wolf form in the middle of a game, which doesn't even cause a stoppage in play.

Scott goes on to become the most popular kid at school and leads his team to The Big Game. Unfortunately, he's also managed to alienate all of his friends and teammates in the process. Finally, he leads the basketball team to a win in The Big Game by playing as himself, rather than in werewolf form.

Recently, this particular bad movie has become somewhat legendary in sports circles. There seems to be a whole cottage industry that has sprung up based on analyzing the basketball scenes in this film. There's a McSweeney's article detailing one coach's strategy for defending the Teen Wolf himself. A clip of the final game montage on YouTube tracks Scott's stats during the game, while the comments include many people wondering about the respective strategies of each team and which players really contributed the most to the Beavers' victory—personally, I'm still a fan of number 45, who not only scored eight points, but also added three critical blocks on the defensive end. Across the internet, you can find dozens of people pointing out how Fox and the actors portraying his teammates don't exactly look like basketball players out on the court.

That's the kind of fun you can only have with a sports movie. Sure, those who have served in the military can point out all of the inconsistencies in the weapons used in a war film, and computer experts wince every time the word "hacker" is used in a movie, but sports give us numbers, statistics, and strategies that give fans topics to argue about year round—and also give us plenty of ways to ridicule some of the sillier scenes in sports movies, which tend to play fast and loose with reality for dramatic effect.

If you're not a sports fan at all, some of the movies in this chapter might not interest you—though a few have significant crossover appeal. On the other hand, if you enjoy trying to figure out why blocking a punch is the exception rather than the rule in *Rocky* films, or why the "Flying V" ever worked for *The Mighty Ducks*, you'll find plenty to love about the films that follow.

ROCKY IV
DIRECTED BY SYLVESTER STALLONE
UNITED ARTISTS, MGM (1985)

I know, I'm cheating a little bit here. *Rocky IV* is part of one of the most successful film franchises in cinematic history and has millions of fans to this day. How can I call it a bad movie? Fair enough: it's really not that bad. But it is incredibly cheesy, and it has everything that bad movie fans love—so I couldn't help but put it in the book.

If you're not familiar with the Rocky series of films, we'll need to cover some ground before we can talk about *Rocky IV,* the fourth film in the franchise. It all began in 1976 when Sylvester Stallone wrote and starred in *Rocky,* a film about a down-on-his-luck club boxer from Philadelphia who happens upon a chance to fight for the world heavyweight championship. Now, starring in your own film can be dangerous—this book has plenty of examples of personal projects gone wrong—but in this case, it worked. *Rocky* was not only a box office hit, but also proved to be a critical success, winning Best Picture and two other Oscars.

That resulted in a series of six films exploring the exploits of boxer Rocky Balboa (Sylvester Stallone). He would go on to actually win the heavyweight championship in *Rocky II* and fight Hulk Hogan and Mr. T in *Rocky III.* The incredibly disappointing

Rocky V is simply bad, while the final film in the franchise, *Rocky Balboa*, was a surprisingly strong way to finish the series after thirty years.

That leaves us to talk about *Rocky IV*. The fourth Rocky film is the most ridiculous of the series, but to many, it's also the most entertaining. It took everything that people loved about the Rocky series, found the furthest distance that those elements could be pushed too, and then went several miles beyond. Add in a healthy amount of Cold War era American patriotism and you have a movie that's more over the top than, well, *Over the Top*.

The story begins right after the ending of *Rocky III*, with Rocky presumably ready to retire after having regained his world championship. Meanwhile, the USSR is promoting their Olympic gold medal winning boxer, Ivan Drago (Dolph Lundgren), who is ready to begin his professional career. Simultaneously, former champion Apollo Creed (Carl Weathers) is finding that he misses the life of professional boxing and arranges to fight an exhibition again Drago.

While Rocky—and everyone else in the film—tell Apollo that he should probably back out of this fight against a much younger and much larger opponent, Apollo is dead set on fighting. Even during the fight, as Apollo is clearly overmatched, he refuses to allow Rocky to throw in the towel. Rocky follows his instructions, and...well, I won't spoil what happens, but chances are that you can see where this is going.

Rocky wants revenge and agrees to fight Drago in Russia on Christmas—against the wishes of his wife, Adrian (Talia Shire). After the requisite training montages, the fight is on. Rocky struggles in the early rounds before beginning to turn things around, and...well, once again, you should see where this is going.

That plot description alone should make it clear that this film is slightly different than the original *Rocky*. No longer are we concerned with the personal struggle of one man against a world that has kept him down. Now it's the United States versus the USSR in a battle that could be to the death. The gritty realism of the first movie's boxing scenes have been replaced with fights in which each fighter throws about two hundred power punches per round and lands approximately ninety-six percent of them to the head. Drago is injected with steroids while Rocky pulls wagons through the Russian wilderness. I never claimed the movie was subtle.

But who needs subtle, anyway? *Rocky IV* may be ridiculous, but it's also amazing from start to finish. There's barely a minute that goes by in this movie without something utterly absurd happening, so you'll rarely feel like you're being let down in the entertainment department. It may not have the award-winning pedigree of *Rocky,* but if you're in the right frame of mind, you'll have a hard time finding a film that's more fun to watch than this one.

WHAT TO WATCH FOR

- Early in the film, Rocky's family gathers to celebrate the birthday of Adrian's brother, Paulie (Burt Young). One of Paulie's gifts is a highly advanced talking robot servant that would be considered a technological marvel today, let alone in 1985.

- Before the fight between Apollo and Drago, both fighters go through the customary ring entrances. In this case, that means that James Brown will sing "Living in America" while a large choreographed dance number engulfs most of the arena. Lundgren does a great job in this scene of portraying an absolutely perplexed Drago, who enters—along with the ring—from below the arena floor.
- The two training montages for Rocky and Drago are shown in tandem, with Rocky's traditional hard work being pitted against Drago's technologically advanced training methods. This ends in the only way it possibly can: with Rocky outrunning the KGB agents assigned to monitor him before climbing a snow-covered mountain.
- Don't walk away from the movie after the climactic fight ends. After the final round, Rocky proceeds to give one of the most important speeches of all time to the Russian crowd. Judging by their reaction, Rocky may have singlehandedly been responsible for ending the Cold War.
- By law, every sports movie in the 1980s had to feature at least one montage, and each montage had to be accompanied by epic music. In *Rocky IV,* we get a driving montage, a training montage, and a boxing montage, so you can expect plenty of rousing anthems. Nothing quite at the level of "Eye of the Tiger," but certainly special in its own right.

RELATED FILMS

As I said above, *Rocky* is legitimately a classic film. If you haven't seen it, it's well worth checking out, even if a boxing movie wouldn't normally be your thing. On the other hand, bad movie fans might enjoy all of the later sequels in the franchise, starting with *Rocky III*. While *Rocky V* is mostly just plain bad, the third film has some silly moments—though not nearly to the level of *Rocky IV*—and the final film in the series—*Rocky Balboa*—features a very old Rocky somehow competing against the current world champion, which is a pretty ridiculous concept in its own right.

PENTATHLON
DIRECTED BY BRUCE MALMUTH
LIVE ENTERTAINMENT (1994)

If you liked Dolph Lundgren as a deadly Russian boxer, you'll love him as a well-rounded East German athlete! *Pentathlon* is the story of Eric Brogar (Dolph Lundgren), one of the world's foremost competitors in the modern pentathlon. For those not familiar with this lesser-known Olympic competition, it's a combination of five different disciplines that are designed to cover all aspects of a "modern" soldier's duties: pistol shooting, fencing, swimming, riding a horse, and running.

Okay, so that's a little outdated—maybe they should add a drone-piloting event—but it's still a tough test, and Brogar is the best. He wins a gold medal in the 1988 Seoul Summer Olympics. Still, Brogar dreams of more, and at the end of the games, he defects to the United States.

This is where things start to fall off the rails a bit for the movie. The film quickly skips ahead several years, and we find out that Brogar is now a drunk who works at a burger joint in Los Angeles. Eventually, his boss (Roger E. Mosley) discovers that he's a former champion, and vows to train him for the 1996 Olympics in Atlanta.

Meanwhile, Brogar's former trainer, Heinrich Mueller (David Soul), is now a terrorist and a leader in the neo-Nazi movement. Mueller is still angry that Brogar defected and decides it's time to get revenge. Simultaneously, Mueller also wants to spring a plot in which he will broadcast a message over cable TV while simultaneously attacking a peace rally, a plan that is sure to bring the world over to his point of view.

When you watch *Pentathlon,* be prepared to watch two films that have been forced to share the same screen—one of which is a fairly mediocre sports film in which Dolph Lundgren attempts to get back into shape in time for the Olympics and a separate film in which neo-Nazis are trying to kill him because one guy wants revenge for some stuff that happened eight years earlier than is in no way related to their political views. It's this second film that gets most of the laughs, as the terrorists try in vain to kill Brogar and his loved ones.

While *Pentathlon* doesn't consistently deliver great moments throughout, there's more than enough to get you to the final scene—and believe me, it's worth the wait. That's when the two divergent plots truly come together in the most absurd way possible, as Brogar attempts to qualify for the USA pentathlon team. Without a doubt, the conclusion has to rank among the three most unlikely finishes to a pentathlon of all time. Will Dolph make the team? You'll have to watch to find out.

OVER THE TOP
DIRECTED BY MENAHEM GOLAN
WARNER BROS. PICTURES (1987)

Is there any one sport that encapsulates the American spirit more than arm wrestling? If you're like me, you can probably think of about a dozen. Still, that didn't stop the creation of *Over the Top*, a film that combines this greatest of sports with another great American pastime: trucking.

Sylvester Stallone stars in this film—which he also co-wrote—as Lincoln Hawk, an arm-wrestling trucker who...well, he drives a truck. And he arm wrestles. His former wife is in the hospital, so she asks Lincoln to pick up his son Michael (David Mendenhall) from the military academy he's attending.

This is the setup for the wacky odd couple section of the movie. Lincoln is a manly man! He drives trucks and arm wrestles! Michael is cultured and doesn't like steak! That's right: the kid coming out of military school is set up to be the effeminate foil for Stallone's character.

The two eventually find common ground, of course, and most of the movie is about the father and son growing closer together. Most of this is accomplished through the magic of arm wrestling, as Lincoln wins matches against other truckers, prepares for the World Arm Wrestling Championships in Las Vegas, and teaches his son how to arm wrestle against other children. Meanwhile, Michael's grandfather is plotting to take him away from Lincoln, using tactics ranging from attempted kidnappings to bribery. At one point, Lincoln runs his truck into the grandfather's mansion in an attempt to get his son back. As brilliant as this plan is, it fails.

Of course, all of these plots converge on the championship tournament. There are a few things you'll need to know about this event:

- Like any movie about an obscure activity, *Over the Top* presents arm wrestling as a mainstream spectator sport. This means there are huge crowds at the World Championships, along with television coverage and hundreds of competitors. Arm wrestling: it's the fastest growing sport in America!

- Apparently, the world of arm wrestling has a trucker division. Who knew that trucking and arm wrestling had such great synergy?
- This tournament is double-elimination. You got that? If you lose once, you will not be eliminated. That means that if a character we're supposed to care about loses, he'll still have one more shot at winning the tournament. I'm sure we won't have to worry about that, but just in case, the film will remind you a couple dozen times during the tournament montage.

If you're looking for reasons to watch this movie, you hardly need to go beyond the premise itself. However, if Stallone as an arm-wrestling trucker isn't enough to get you interested, it's worth noting that *Over the Top* also earned three prestigious nominations from the Golden Raspberry Awards. That included two Razzie wins for Mendenhall, who won both Worst Supporting Actor and Worst New Star for his portrayal of Michael. It's hard to say if this is really Mendenhall's fault, though: he wasn't given much to work with.

The ending is just as cliché as you expect it to be, with everything and anything that could go right for Hawk coming together. He gets the son, the grandfather realizes he's actually the greatest thing since sliced bread, he wins money, he wins *more* money, and he's ready to live the American dream by starting his own trucking company. Thank you, arm wrestling—you've brought yet another family together!

THE FAN
DIRECTED BY TONY SCOTT
MANDALAY ENTERTAINMENT, SCOTT FREE
PRODUCTIONS, TRISTAR PICTURES (1996)

Stories about people who take things just a little too seriously can sometimes be fun. There are plenty of movies or television shows that have explored the idea of the obsessed fan who just doesn't know when to stop. It's a story that tends to resonate, because we're all passionate about different things—and in any fandom, there's always a few people who straddle the line between loving their subject of affection and becoming downright scary in their devotion.

In the case of *The Fan,* the subject in question is baseball: certainly something more than a few people take way too seriously—for proof, you need only tune into the local sports talk radio station during the summer. The baseball fan in question is Gil Renard (Robert De Niro), a man whose life is falling apart around him. He's a terrible father, has divorced from his son's mother, and might even be losing his job as a knife salesman. But there's one part of his life that he's still passionate about: the San Francisco Giants.

The upcoming season is an exciting one, as the Giants have just signed superstar outfielder Bobby Rayburn (Wesley Snipes), who is played as a virtual Barry Bonds stand-in. But things don't

get off to a good star for Rayburn, as he struggles with injuries and fails to live up to the expectations of the fans. Part of
the problem is his cold relationship with Juan Primo (Benicio del
Toro), the other star on the Giants. Rayburn had always worn
#11 during his career, but Primo just won't give it up, forcing
Rayburn to wear a different jersey.

Seeing the conflict between Rayburn and Primo, Gil quickly
figures out that this is the reason why the new star of his favorite team isn't performing well. He takes the step any good fan
would: he murders Primo using one of the knives he is so bad at
selling. Now, you might think that's a bit of an overreaction, but
what do you know, it works! Rayburn breaks out of his slump
and all is right again in the world of the Giants.

Gil knows he did a good job, so he rewards himself by spying on
Rayburn's beach house. Amazingly, this creepy and invasive act
actually manages to save the life of Rayburn's son, who was playing in the ocean and nearly drowns. Rayburn thanks Gil for being
in the right place at the right time and *totally* not spying on him.
But Gil's still not pleased, because Rayburn says that the death of a
teammate he didn't get along with perfectly wasn't the best thing
to ever happen to his career. Instead, it made him realize there were
more important things in life than baseball and fickle fans.

That's when the movie really takes off. Gil kidnaps Rayburn's
son, and somehow manages to stay one step ahead of both the multimillionaire baseball player and the cops. This eventually leads to
a confrontation at a Giants game, where we learn an important
lesson: if a crazy fan kidnaps your son and demands that you hit
a home run, it's very important that everyone focus on hitting the

home run as the likely way in which your child will be saved, rather than focusing on silly little things like police investigations.

The Fan has a strong cast and certainly doesn't suffer from the kinds of poor production values enjoyed by many of the movies I've recommended, but the absurd plot more than makes up for this. You'll be entertained by the antics of De Niro's character, which start out as sad and obsessive and quickly rise to complete insanity. Characters react in ways that are wildly inappropriate for the situations they find themselves in, the thriller-aspects of the story consistently fall flat, and the climax of the movie is about as plausible as the Cubs winning a World Series sometime this decade.

D3: THE MIGHTY DUCKS
DIRECTED BY ROBERT LIEBERMAN
AVNET/KERNER PRODUCTIONS, WALT DISNEY
PICTURES (1996)

If you're not familiar with the Mighty Ducks series of films, here's what you need to know. *The Mighty Ducks* was a fairly strong family film about a lawyer named Gordon Bombay (Emilio Estevez), who is losing control of his life. Sentenced to community service, he's forced to coach a peewee hockey team made up of a ragtag bunch of misfits. They laugh, they learn from each other, and they ultimately win a state championship over the designated Evil Team, the Hawks.

The first sequel in the series—*D2: The Mighty Ducks*—basically followed the same format. Bombay takes up minor league hockey in an attempt to get to the NHL, but is injured and forced back into coaching. He somehow finds himself as the coach for Team USA at the Jr. Goodwill Games, and—who would have thought—the Ducks are welcomed along to form the core of that team as well, with a few players from around the country joining them. They once again have their ups and downs, everyone learns some valuable lessons, and Team USA wins the gold medals over the designated Evil Team—Iceland, a country not known for its hockey prowess.

Where the first sequel was simply a retread of the first movie, *D3: The Mighty Ducks* is certainly a different film. Estevez had little interest in appearing in the movie, but was convinced to take on a small role while still being billed as one of the film's stars. The result is that Bombay is written out of most of the film, and the Ducks are sent off to Eden Hall, a snooty prep school with a powerhouse hockey program. The idea is that the Ducks will serve as the Junior Varsity team for the school, and that the entire team will be given full scholarships in exchange.

Inevitably, conflict occurs. The Ducks don't really fit in as a whole, and the team rebels against their new leader, Coach Orion (Jeffrey Nordling). He wants them to act like a hockey team instead of relying on gimmicky plays and practical jokes. The nerve of that guy! Nobody takes this harder than Charlie Conway (Joshua Jackson), who leaves the team to do more important things, like hang out at an amusement park.

The Mighty Ducks franchise died a quiet death after this film and it's easy to see why. One might expect a hockey movie to feature a fair amount of hockey, but until the climax of the movie, hockey scenes are few and far between. Instead, the focus is on practical jokes between the Ducks and their new rivals, the school's Varsity team. The Ducks, as it turns out, may be able to win an international competition against the best young hockey players in the world, but they're no match for the JV squads at other prep schools.

But that doesn't stop this one from ending the same way these movies always do. The kids learn some lessons, everyone decides to work together, and on the day of the big game, the Ducks once again triumph over the designated Evil Team—Varsity.

This one might not be a sure recommendation for the average bad movie fan. It's actually fairly boring at times, despite the fact that there are plenty of ridiculous moments. That said, fans of the earlier Mighty Ducks films or kids sports movies in general will have fun watching just how far this once beloved franchise fell. There are skating shenanigans, some painfully bad jokes, and a couple of references to the fact that the Anaheim Mighty Ducks were actually named after the hockey team portrayed in these films. It's still better than the animated cartoon—the one that featured walking, talking, hockey-playing alien ducks—but that's not really saying much, is it?

THE CUTTING EDGE 3: CHASING THE DREAM
DIRECTED BY STUART GILLARD
MGM (2008)

The Cutting Edge was a fairly popular 1992 romantic comedy about a female figure skater (Moira Kelly) who takes on the most unlikely of partners for her next Olympic run: an ice hockey player (D. B. Sweeney), who had his career cut short by an eye injury. It's a predictable film, but it's competently made and perfectly enjoyable.

Surprisingly, this film spawned a franchise that has so far included four films. None of the sequels were released in theaters. Instead, they were all produced for the ABC Family cable network, with even the first sequel, *The Cutting Edge: Going for the Gold,* coming more than a decade after the original was released.

While it's likely that any of these made-for-TV movies would be worthy of inclusion, the one I've personally seen is *The Cutting Edge 3: Chasing the Dream.* This film offers a number of incredible twists on the plot formula used by the original film. You see, this time it's a male figure skater (Zach Conroy, played by Matt Lanter) who is stuck without a female partner, and it's a female hockey player (Alejandra Delgado, played by Francia Raisa) who he grooms to be his new partner. Bet you never saw that one coming.

The plot itself is as simple as you'd imagine: Delgado isn't really ready to perform at the Olympic level, but she has a lot of raw talent. Through the use of magical training montages, she manages to improve incredibly quickly, and after some trials and tribulations, they win The Big Competition while falling for each other in the process.

But that's not enough to carry ninety minutes of action, so there's plenty of other drama thrown in to pad out the film. There's the injured partner who used to date Conroy and is now going to marry their estranged coach. There's a Russian skater who wanders in and out of the plot and an arrogant pair of rivals who do evil things, such as rooting for our heroes to fall during their routines. Throw in Alejandra's protective family and you've got more subplots than you can shake a hockey stick at. The film also throws in a few obligatory references to the original film, including bringing in a coach who is supposed to be the daughter of the two main characters from *The Cutting Edge*—ignoring the fact that since the first film took place during the 1988 Olympics, any child of theirs would likely still be a teenager at the time of this movie.

The Cutting Edge 3: Chasing the Dream isn't among the top bad movies on my list, but it definitely works if you're looking for a sports film or something with a Winter Olympics theme. There's no doubt that it's delightfully cheesy throughout—I especially enjoyed Ben Hollingsworth in his limited screen time as Jason Bright, one half of the main rival team that our heroes compete against—and there are more than a few moments that will surprise you, including a particularly memorable incident in the middle of Zach and Alejandra's first competitive routine. Those skates are sharp, so knowing exactly where your partner is at all times is probably a good idea.

Animated Titanic Movies

I know what you're thinking: how can there be an entire section of this book devoted to animated movies about the Titanic? To be fair, it's not a very long section: there are only two movies covered. However, these movies are so different from anything else in this book—and so similar to each other—that they deserved their own little corner all to themselves.

Both animated Titanic movies are Italian productions, and both feature plenty of animals along for the ride along with the human passengers. From there, though, the two films head in very different directions, and true bad movie fans will want to be familiar with both. Which film is worse? That's a subject that always generates heated debate. One thing is for certain, though: you'll never look at the story of the Titanic the same way again.

TITANIC: THE LEGEND GOES ON
DIRECTED BY CAMILLO TETI
TITANIC CARTOONS (2000)

If you were a fan of James Cameron's *Titanic*, but thought it would be even better if it were animated and featured talking animals, *Titanic: The Legend Goes On* is the film for you. This Italian effort features many of the same themes that are present in the Cameron film: an unlikely romance between two young lovers, a story told in flashback, and plenty of tension between passengers of different classes (and species).

That's not to suggest that there's nothing original in this version of the Titanic story. This time, a boy named William (Mark Ashworth) is the rich one, and the girl, Angelica (Lisa Russo), is struggling with her adoptive family. Strangely enough, William has a nanny who once gave up a daughter, and has no idea what became of her. Do I really need to spoil the twist here?

Throughout the film, the many talking animals (including stereotypical Mexican mice, as well as various cats and dogs) help William and Angelica find each other. At some point, there's a rapping dog. On the Titanic, it's party time!

Of course, our couple comes together just in time for the Titanic to hit an iceberg. The drama of the most famous ship disaster plays out much as it has in every Titanic film you've ever seen: the rich and famous passengers have the best of it, most of the lower-class voyagers are stuck below deck, and there aren't enough lifeboats to save everyone. But since this is a kid's movie, we need to have a somewhat happy ending: Angelica is reunited with her mother, and rather than allowing him to die, Jack—I mean, William!—is saved at the last minute. The movie ends with a montage allowing us to see that all of our favorite characters and animals lived happily ever after, apparently un-affected by the horrors they just witnessed.

As I'm writing this, *Titanic: The Legend Goes On* is currently ranked #1 on IMDB's Bottom 100 list, marking it the worst movie ever as voted by users of their website. Certainly, it's an incredibly bland rip-off of *Titanic,* the animation is subpar, and—in case you'd forgotten—there's a rapping dog. But I hate to break it to you, read-ers: this isn't even the worst animated Titanic film I've seen. How could someone create a movie worse than this? Read on, if you dare...

THE LEGEND OF THE TITANIC
DIRECTED BY ORLANDO CORRADI
AND KIM J. OK
HOLLYWOOD GANG PRODUCTIONS, ITB,
AND MONDO TV (1999)

Yes, this is the animated Titanic film that is often described as "even worse than that other animated Titanic movie." In *The Legend of the Titanic,* an aging mouse named Top Connors (Sean Patrick Lovett) tells his grandchildren the true story of the Titanic—one that has a few interesting details you're probably unaware of.

So Bad, It's Good

It seems that our narrator mouse was put in charge of the many immigrant mice on board the Titanic. Of course, there are also plenty of humans on board, including Elizabeth (Jane Alexander), a wealthy young woman who is due to marry a scheming whaler named Evarard Maltravers (Gregory Snegoff). While Maltravers pretends to have interest in Elizabeth, he's really more interested in gaining the whaling rights currently owned by Elizabeth's father.

So far, this sounds a lot like most Titanic tales with a few talking mice thrown in, but it seems that Conners' "true story" about the Titanic is quite different than the one you're familiar with. Let's try running down the laundry list of minor changes made by the writers:

- Maltravers arranges for the sinking of the ship by working with a gang of sharks. Not just any sharks, mind you, but the very worst kind: shark criminals!
- The sharks can't sink the ship on their own, so they fool a naive octopus named Tentacles into throwing an iceberg in front of the Titanic as part of a contest to see who can throw large objects the farthest.
- Realizing what he has done, Tentacles uses his immense strength to hold together the Titanic as long as possible in order to give the ship's passengers enough time to flee onto lifeboats.
- With the help of some whales and dolphins, everyone survives, including the ship's captain.

To recap: the Titanic was sunk by a foolish Octopus who was unwittingly following the orders of a greedy whaling baron, but it was ultimately okay, because nobody died. Just like in real life!

While *The Legend of the Titanic* gleefully ignores history and arguably insults the memory of all those who died on the Titanic, that's far from the only ridiculous aspect to this film. When a mouse is understandably questioned about his love for a human woman, he simply replies that he's "not a racist." When Elizabeth is upset about having to marry Maltravers, she finds that magic moonbeams allow her to talk to levitating dolphins. A mouse dies in the effort to repair the Titanic's communication systems, but later returns for the end-of-movie celebration. It's fun for the whole family!

While *Titanic: The Legend Goes On* is certainly a worthy entry into the bad movie Parthenon, there's no doubt in my mind that *The Legend of the Titanic* clearly outpaces it to become the worst animated movie about the Titanic that I've had the pleasure to watch. As an added bonus, if this film leaves you with the urge to learn more about these characters, you can always check out *In Search of the Titanic*, a sequel that features Tentacles and some other returning characters searching for the Titanic's wreckage.

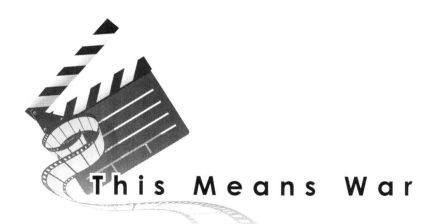

This Means War

*S*aving *Private Ryan*. *Braveheart*. *Schindler's List*. Some of the greatest and most popular films of all time are set against the backdrop of wars and it's easy to see why. A war provides drama on numerous levels: there's the immediate life-and-death struggle that comes with being in the middle of a battle, the emotional toll this takes on the combatants, and the terror of their loved ones back at home. If there's an important cause to fight for and a rousing speech or two, you've got a recipe for success.

Even in movies that aren't strictly about war, battles—especially gun fights—are a quick and easy way to add a little drama and action into an otherwise lifeless film. It's an easy way to throw danger into the mix for the hero, or to give him (or her) a chance to show off their bravery, courage, or ability to blow things up. To paraphrase the character Michael Scott from *The Office*, the most exciting thing that can happen in a movie is someone having a gun. You can't top it...except, maybe, if a lot of people have guns.

All of the movies in this chapter feature battles, wars, or a whole lot of guns. Of course, no two battles are alike: there are humans battling humans, robots battling robots, humans shooting at robots and aliens, and even Uncle Jesse fighting an army led by a hermaphroditic Gene Simmons. Don't worry, you won't have to wait—we'll jump right into that last one first.

NEVER TOO YOUNG TO DIE
DIRECTED BY GIL BETTMAN
PAUL ENTERTAINMENT (1986)

Ladies and gentlemen: John Stamos. You probably know him either as Uncle Jesse from *Full House,* or perhaps as "that guy who was in a few things, but is most famous as Uncle Jesse from *Full House.*" But believe it or not, Stamos did have a career before he teamed up with the Olsen twins. After getting his start on television—which remains to this day the arena in which he's had the most success—Stamos was picked as the heroic lead for the action/adventure film *Never Too Young to Die.*

The story follows Lance Stargrove (Stamos)—a college gymnast who wishes his father would pay more attention to him. Unbeknownst to Lance, his father is actually a secret agent who died while battling one of the most interesting movie villains ever: Gene Simmons as Velvet Von Ragnar, a hermaphroditic crime boss who plans to poison the city's water supply. Need I say more?

The plot here is actually rather straightforward. Stargrove figures out that his father's death wasn't an accident and runs into some of Ragnar's thugs. He eventually finds a way to take up his father's mantle and fight back, with the ultimate goal of taking down Ragnar once and for all. Along the way, he meets Danja Deering (Vanity), who serves as Stamos' regulation love interest. They spend most of their time fighting Ragnar's ridiculous minions and attempting to foil his dastardly plans.

If John Stamos doesn't strike you as a prototypical action hero, your instincts are probably right on the mark. During a critical monologue late in the movie, in which Stargrove taunts one of Ragnar's lieutenants, Stamos is essentially playing the Uncle Jesse character he'd become famous for, right down to mugging for the camera. The fact that this leads into a typical 80s action sequence with two armies battling each other and plentiful explosions makes this movie a truly surreal experience.

The final confrontation between Stamos and Simmons is appropriately bizarre and the way in which Stargrove saves the day at the last possible second is the perfect way to end the film. If you're a fan of action movie clichés, ridiculous plot contrivances, and everything that makes so many pine for the 1980s, *Never Too Young to Die* will leave you thoroughly entertained.

ROBOWAR
DIRECTED BY BRUNO MATTEI
FLORA FILM (1989)

Another movie from the portfolio of Reb Brown (star of *Space Mutiny*, if you'll recall), *Robowar* claims to be directed by Vincent Dawn, but that's just a pseudonym for Bruno Mattei, the visionary behind films such as *Strike Commando* and *Hell of the Living Dead*, both of which were also directed under the Dawn name. He's also behind movies like *Porno Holocaust* and the Italian movie known as *Terminator 2*—which has nothing to do with the film you know by this name—so you know going in that you're getting a quality product.

Robowar tells the story of Major Murphy Black (Reb Brown), who is leading a group of soldiers—the group has a colorful nickname, but I'll allow you to discover that for yourself—that have been recruited by the CIA to rescue prisoners being held by terrorists somewhere in Central America. But their job is going to be a lot harder than they think, thanks to a little detail that the government neglected to tell the team—there's a deadly robot that they'll need to disable and retrieve in order to complete the mission. In fact, the team really isn't told anything about their mission, except that they'll be landing on an island.

Considering the lack of information, it's no surprise that the team spends a lot of time walking around the island figuring out exactly what they're supposed to be doing. Oh, they'll occasionally fire hundreds of bullets into the foliage, and Reb is sure to scream a lot—as is his nature—but the movie doesn't really pick up until they meet Omega One: the ultimate killing machine.

Omega One isn't exactly the most intimidating villain ever. The movie occasionally shows us the high-tech visual interface that the robot uses to view the world, which consists of a low-resolution camera with a yellow filter and a targeting crosshair. Omega One also talks a lot, though it mainly says the same few words over and over again, including one that sounds like "greasy."

Even after the killer robot appears, there's still a little time for human drama, as Reb and company rescue a woman from some guerrilla fighters—once again, firing hundreds of times in order to kill just a few enemies. She directs them to a nearby village that they free from those same guerrillas through the power of firing as often as possible at anything that moves.

It's around this point when Omega One shows up to do some actual killing. Over and over again, Reb's team fires hundreds of bullets into the jungle in the hopes of maybe getting lucky and hitting the robot. Amazingly, this strategy is largely ineffective, as the robot manages to pick them off one by one. This leads to an extended battle between Reb Brown and the robot, which takes on added importance due to a ridiculous plot twist that tries—unsuccessfully—to add a little emotional resonance to the fighting.

If the above description didn't make it clear, this movie is a shameless rip-off of *Predator*, with many scenes being taken virtually shot for shot from the Arnold Schwarzenegger classic. There are only two notable differences between the films: first,

Robowar has a robot instead of an alien hunter, and secondly, *Predator* is better in every way that one film can possibly outshine another. Other than those tiny distinctions, though, you're basically watching one of the greatest action movies of the decade.

That's not to say that *Robowar* isn't tremendously entertaining. From Reb Brown's signature enthusiasm to the ridiculous robot villain and the horrendous dialogue present throughout, *Robowar* never stops delivering a steady stream of bad movie goodness. If you're a big fan of Brown's or just cheesy action movies in general, this one can't be missed.

ROBOT JOX
DIRECTED BY STUART GORDON
EMPIRE PICTURES, ALTAR
PRODUCTIONS (1989)

Imagine a world with no war. Now, imagine that in this world, there are still plenty of situations in which nations cannot peacefully resolve their differences. What's the logical solution? Hold giant robot battles.

That's the reality in the world of *Robot Jox*, a science-fiction/action movie that's set fifty years after a nuclear war. The "jox" in question are the men and women who pilot the giant robots into battle, where the winning side often claims disputed territory for their nations: the Russian Confederation and the Western Market, which more or less acts as a stand-in for the United States.

The main character is Achilles (Gary Graham), a successful jockey for the Western Market who is about to enter the tenth and final battle of his career, after which his contract will be fulfilled. He's about to go into the arena against Alexander (Paul Koslo), one of the most successful Russian jockeys of all time. Alexander has not only won all nine fights in his career, but he's killed all of the Western jockeys he's been up against.

Alexander and Achilles get into a heated duel, and Alexander launches a weapon that heads off course and toward the crowd in attendance. Achilles tries to block the missile, but instead collapses into the bleachers, killing numerous spectators. This raises many questions, not the least of which is why you'd have a live audience for a battle between gigantic robots who are using large and dangerous weapons against each other.

Given the highly unusual circumstances of the ending to this international giant robot battle, the officials—yes, there are referees who wear the same kinds of uniforms you'd expect to see them wear in a football game—order a rematch. Achilles believes he's fulfilled his contract, while the Market wants him to fight Alexander one last time. Will he come out of retirement or will another hero emerge?

During the movie, we spend most of our time behind the scenes at the Western Market's Robot Fighting Ministry—probably not the official name—where several plots emerge. Achilles is aided by robot designer Matsumoto (Danny Kamekona), who is constantly innovating weapons and defenses designed to give his side a leg up. Strategic advice comes courtesy of Tex Conway (Michael Alldredge), a retired jockey who might be hiding some secrets from his past. We also meet many aspiring jockeys, including Athena, who expects to pick up the mantle when Achilles retires. Finally, there's a mole who is secretly working for the Confederation, because...well, in these kinds of stories, there's always a mole. It was basically a legal requirement during the Cold War.

Robot Jox is a stupid movie, but it's also incredibly fun. With giant robots fighting each other, how could it not be? The battle scenes are both epic and ridiculous, and the characters are all caricatures of themselves, but with a movie like this, you won't want it any other way.

All of this leads to *Robot Jox*'s infamous ending, which I won't spoil here. Suffice it to say that while it doesn't quite beat the end of *Rocky IV* in terms of inspirational war-ending gestures, it's certainly right up there, and marks a one hundred and eighty degree turn from the tone of the film in the beginning up until the final few seconds.

OPERATION WARZONE
DIRECTED BY DAVID A. PRIOR
AIP HOME VIDEO INC. (1988)

Operation Warzone is a low-budget Vietnam War tale. Surviving a Viet Cong ambush, three US Army soldiers mount a rescue mission to retrieve two undercover agents. Those agents, in turn, are looking for The General—a man who has evidence that could break open an illegal arms deal that involves corrupt Army officers and a Pentagon official. Led by Sergeant Holt (Fritz Matthews), the men must fight to survive not only attacks from Viet Cong soldiers, but also corrupt members of the US military who want to stop them before they can take their evidence public.

Filled with plenty of action scenes and explosions, *Operation Warzone* could have easily been forgotten as just another one of the dozens of Vietnam War movies that came out in the 1980s. However, this movie earns special recognition due to the interesting musical choices made throughout the film. Gunfights regularly occur with upbeat and cheerful music that seems entirely unconnected to what's happening in the movie. Trust me: you'll come for the action, but it'll be this film's amazing music cues that will have you laughing throughout.

In particular, there's a scene where two soldiers end an argument by getting into a long fistfight. There's nothing particularly wrong with the action on screen, but the accompanying music would be more appropriate for a triumphant scene at the end of a romantic movie when the couple finally shares their first dance than a brutal brawl in the jungles of Vietnam. Perhaps it should come as no surprise that the composer for *Operation Warzone* was none other than Steve McClintock—the same man who provided the music for *Space Mutiny.*

ALIEN OPPONENT

DIRECTED BY COLIN THEYS

SYNTHETIC CINEMA INTERNATIONAL, VIJAYA CINE ENTERPRISES (2010)

Starring Jeremy London and "Rowdy" Roddy Piper, *Alien Opponent* is about the aftermath of a UFO crash that takes place in a junkyard. The owner of the junkyard is killed by his wife's mother around the same time, which makes for a convenient alibi. It also gives both the widow (Ashley Bates) and her mother Rita (Hilma Falkowski) the chance to collect on a huge life insurance policy...but only if they can recover the body.

Their plan: offer a cash prize to anyone who can get in, grab the body, and bring it back to the family. That turns the junkyard into an all-out battle, as the alien sets up defenses in order to hold out until it can repair its ship, while dozens of hopeful bounty hunters—led by Piper and London—arrive in the hopes of collecting the reward. Of course, most of them are woefully underprepared, leading to plenty of gruesome deaths along the way. There are also numerous subplots, as each person who wants to kill the alien—and there are a lot of them—has a story to tell.

A concept like this is guaranteed to lead to a cheesy film, and *Alien Opponent* doesn't disappoint. The entire film is ridiculous, and while parts of the film clearly show a level of self-awareness, it never turns into a parody. If you've ever wanted to see people killed by an electronic land shark or a zombie Roddy Piper, this is the movie for you.

Quick Picks

Occasionally, you'll hear the title or concept of a movie and immediately know that it's going to be hilariously awful: no further explanation required. The following films belong in this book with only minimal comment.

NIGHT OF THE LEPUS
DIRECTED BY WILLIAM F. CLAXTON
A.C. LYLES PRODUCTIONS (1972)

Brave humans defend themselves from rabbits. Not just ordinary rabbits, mind you: giant rabbits that grow to the size of cattle. This would have been more frightening had they not used men in rabbit suits and obvious models to create the illusion of monstrous rabbits.

DEATH BED: THE BED THAT EATS
DIRECTED BY GEORGE BARRY
CULT EPICS (1977)

A demon-possessed bed eats those who try to sleep in it—at least you can't say the title isn't accurate. Created in the 1970s, it wasn't released until a DVD was created in 2003.

SHOWGIRLS
DIRECTED BY PAUL VERHOEVEN
UNITED ARTISTS, VEGAS PRODUCTIONS
(1995)

One of the bigger critical flops of all time, and notable for being a mainstream NC-17 release, *Showgirls* has attained surprising success in the world of home video. It stars Elizabeth Berkley as a young woman who wants to be a Las Vegas showgirl. While I thought the best way to review this movie would be to quote its most famous line—"Everybody got AIDS and shit"—a friend suggested the following summary: "Fish, barrel, chick from Saved by the Bell."

TWO FRONT TEETH
DIRECTED BY JAMIE NASH AND DAVID
THOMAS SCKRABULIS ROAST BEAST LLC
(2006)

This film chronicles a Christmas story about the fight to stop Clausferatu—the vampire pretender to Santa Claus' seat in North Pole. There's a battle between evil elves and ninja nuns, and the movie ends with an epic martial arts battle between Santa and his undead counterpart. Happy holidays!

FROM JUSTIN TO KELLY
DIRECTED BY ROBERT ISCOVE
19 ENTERTAINMENT (2003)

Considered to be one of the worst musicals ever filmed, this spring break party movie stars American Idol winner Kelly Clarkson and runner-up Justin Guarini as an unlikely couple. A note to future filmmakers: just because someone can sing, that doesn't mean they can act. For further case studies, watch *Glitter* or *Crossroads*.

THE WICKER MAN
DIRECTED BY NEIL LABUTE
MILLENNIUM FILMS, SATURN FILMS, WARNER
BROS. PICTURES (2006)

The 1973 film *The Wicker Man* is considered a horror classic. The 2006 remake that stars Nicolas Cage is not. If you don't want to watch the whole thing, there are plenty of highlight reels available online. *Oh god, not the bees!*

Odds and Ends

The following films didn't fit neatly into any of the other categories in the book. That's not to say that they're unclassifiable: they include horror films, TV movies and dramas, among others. But as I only had one or two of each of these film types in the book, it made sense to group the rest of the films together, rather than shoehorning them into other categories.

That said, there's certainly a lot of star power in this section. In the pages to come, you'll find movies starring Tom Hanks, Fred Savage, Hulk Hogan, and at least two superstars from the world of music. There are independent pictures made on tiny budgets and big budget films that were designed to springboard careers. Some of these films talk about serious issues, while others are about killing giant fish or beating people at video games. The one thing they have in common is that they're all welcome choices on bad movie night.

THE WIZARD
DIRECTED BY TODD HOLLAND
UNIVERSAL PICTURES (1989)

The year was 1989. Nintendo was the undisputed worldwide champion of home video game consoles, and the brand was quickly becoming synonymous with the entire industry. Everyone was looking for ways to incorporate Nintendo into other products: cartoons, action figures, breakfast cereals, and yes, even movies.

That's basically the story behind *The Wizard,* a film that amounts to little more than a hundred-minute commercial for Nintendo products. This was a movie squarely aimed at achieving two goals: getting kids who play Nintendo into movie theaters, and then showing them as many desirable Nintendo products as possible.

Okay, that last paragraph might be selling this movie a little short. *The Wizard* may be loaded with product placement, but it at least manages to tell a somewhat coherent story at the same time. It also features a rather impressive cast, which brought the film a dash of legitimacy when it was released. Director Todd Holland even managed to create a few touching moments that had little to do with video games—not an easy task when you're trying to push copies of *Ninja Gaiden* at the same time.

That said, there's no doubting that *The Wizard* belongs in a book about bad movies. The film begins with an introduction to Jimmy Woods (Luke Edwards), a young boy who is suffering from some sort of mental disorder. The way the character is portrayed has led many to speculate that Jimmy was meant to have a disorder on the autism spectrum—however, this is never stated in the film—but the fact that his behavior is said to have changed dramatically when his twin sister died might suggest some sort of post-traumatic stress disorder instead. Either way, Jimmy has mostly withdrawn from the world, refusing to communicate with those around him—other than to say "California"—and frequently run away from home.

While Jimmy lives with his mother and stepfather, his two older half-brothers Corey (Fred Savage) and Nick (Christian Slater) live with their father (Beau Bridges). Corey is particularly upset with the way Jimmy is being treated and runs away with Jimmy in an attempt to bring him to California. Along the way, they meet Haley (Jenny Lewis), a girl who is impressed by Jimmy's prodigious talent for playing Nintendo games and suggests that he compete in Video Armageddon, a Nintendo tournament that will award fifty thousand dollars to the winner.

Much of the film is devoted to two parallel plot lines. Jimmy, Corey, and Haley travel toward the tournament, hustling gamers along the way to raise money for their trip. Meanwhile, Nick and his father try to track down the kids, hoping to find them before Putnam (Will Seltzer), a bounty hunter who has been hired by Jimmy's mother and stepfather to bring him back home.

Along the way, the film finds every excuse possible to fit Nintendo into the plot. Of course, Jimmy needs to play games in order to help fund their trip, but that's not nearly enough screen time, so there's also a montage of him training on dozens of different games in preparation for the tournament. Meanwhile, Nick just happened to bring his NES on the road with him, and he and his father grow closer together while playing video games.

After some hijinks and shenanigans—of course this movie has shenanigans—all of the characters arrive at Video Armageddon at virtually the same time to see Jimmy try to win the tournament. It should go without saying that the outcome is never in doubt—try getting one of your friends to bet that Mora, a character who hadn't yet appeared in the film, will win in the finals—but there's still a dramatic finish that comes down to the final seconds. The movie actually ends on a scene that doesn't reference video games at all, and provides a touching conclusion to Jimmy's story.

Yes, this is a bad movie, and it's one that was made solely to sell video games to impressionable young children, but it's also a movie with heart: you can tell that the director at least *tried* to turn this into a legitimate film. *The Wizard* may be little more than one long Nintendo ad, but at least it's fairly entertaining—and that's more than you can say for most Super Bowl commercials.

FUN FACTS

- At the time of the film's release, Super Mario Bros. 3 had not yet been released in North America, though it had long been available for the NES in Japan. This meant that *The Wizard* marked the first time most viewers in the United States and Canada had ever seen footage of the game—one of the movie's major selling points.

- Jenny Lewis, who played the part of Haley, is now best known as a musician. Lewis was one of the founding members of the band Rilo Kiley, and has also had a successful solo career.

WHAT TO WATCH FOR

- One of the most memorable moments in this film comes with the first appearance of Lucas, the greatest threat to Jimmy's video game dominance. This scene includes the classic line in which Lucas declares his love for the Power Glove, one I won't spoil for those new to *The Wizard*. It's another blatant—and hilarious—example of product placement in the film, made all the more entertaining when one considers that the Power Glove was a flop as an NES accessory.
- On the verge of being captured by Putnam and having their dreams of video game glory dashed, Haley realizes she needs to act fast. She screams, points to Putnam, and delivers a line that can best be described as extremely awkward for a children's movie that mostly served as a commercial for Nintendo products. Again, no spoilers— you'll know it when you see it.
- The climax of the movie takes place at Video Armageddon, the championship event where Jimmy must face off against Lucas one last time. From the overly enthusiastic

host to the chase scene that feels like it was designed as an advertisement for the Universal Studios tour, everything about theses scenes is deliciously over-the-top.

MEGA PIRANHA
DIRECTED BY ERIC FROSBERG
THE GLOBAL ASYLUM (2010)

It would be impossible to cover the world of B-movie filmmaking without including at least one film by The Asylum, the premier producer of low-budget science fiction films and "mockbusters"—a concept I'll dig a little deeper into in a moment. Since so many of these films will either annoy you or entertain you for the same reasons, I wanted to include just one of them in this book, though I'll be sure to list a few of their other infamous works along the way. With all due apologies to *Mega Shark vs. Giant Octopus*—which includes possibly the greatest scene ever written in Asylum history, in which a shark leaps out of the ocean to eat a passing airplane—I've chosen my personal favorite to talk about: *Mega Piranha*.

To better understand The Asylum, we need to talk about mockbusters: films designed to capitalize on the hype around a major motion picture release. The idea is simple: if there's a highly anticipated film coming to theaters, simply create a movie with a similar theme—and often a similar name as well—that can cash in on the hype of the bigger release. This can happen in two ways: uninformed consumers accidentally pick up your movie instead of the actual blockbuster, or fans who want more of what they've just seen might watch your movie to continue getting the movie experience they now crave.

While this concept dates back to at least the 1950s, there's no doubt that The Asylum has perfected the art over the last few years. While they don't exclusively create mockbusters, these are the films they're best known for. Just a few of their most notable releases include the following (with the film being "copied" in parenthesis):

- *Transmorphers* (*Transformers*)
- *Battle of Los Angeles* (*Battle: Los Angeles*)
- *American Warships* (*Battleship*)
- *Paranormal Entity* (*Paranormal Activity*)
- *Abraham Lincoln vs. Zombies* (*Abraham Lincoln: Vampire Hunter*)

As you can see, The Asylum isn't restricted to any one genre of film: if you have a big movie scheduled for release, you can expect to see a similar Asylum movie in the pipeline. To their credit, these mockbusters almost always feature original stories that aren't related to those in the movies they echo, and the business model apparently works quite well: The Asylum is known for staying under some very tight budgets, and it's been said that they've never lost money on a movie they've produced.

In the case of *Mega Piranha*, the movie being "mocked" was *Piranha 3D*, the 2010 remake of the 1978 horror film *Piranha*.

Mega Piranha was made for the SyFy Network, and actually came out a few months before *Piranha 3D*, as that film ended up facing a few months worth of delays before being released. The production of *Mega Piranha* was actually somewhat more complicated than the typically fast schedule used by The Asylum, as much of the filming was done on location in Belize.

Given the title, you've probably already guessed that this movie deals with some rather large piranhas. The story begins in Venezuela, where some genetically enhanced piranhas have been released from an American scientific installation. Plenty of early deaths let us know that these fish—which are currently just a little bit larger than your typical piranha—mean business. After high-ranking diplomats from the United States and Venezuela die in one such attack, American special forces agent Jason Fitch (Paul Logan) is sent to investigate by Secretary of State Bob Grady (Barry Williams, best known as Greg Brady of *The Brady Bunch*—see what they did there?), as there are fears that the attack was the work of terrorists, militants, or other no-good types.

Meanwhile, a group of scientists are already mounting an investigation of their own, led by genetics researchers Sarah Monroe (played by 80s pop star Tiffany). Back at the lab, Monroe and her team figure out a startling fact: the piranhas are growing exponentially, doubling in size every couple of days. She tells Fitch the truth so that he can forward her findings to Colonel Antonio Diaz (David Labiosa), the Venezuelan military official also taking part in the investigation. While Fitch is increasingly certain that piranhas are behind the attack, Diaz vehemently opposes the idea until he literally has one of the giant fish on his desk.

From here, the plot quickly escalates. The piranhas continue to grow and find bigger targets, eventually attacking battle- ships and major cities. How does a piranha attack a city, you ask? It jumps out of the water and crashes into a building, of course. It then becomes a race against time to see if our heroes can come up with a way to stop the fish before whale-sized pi- ranhas destroy Miami.

But let's face it: you're not watching *Mega Piranha* in order to follow along with the nuances of the plot. This film features the triple crown of bad movie hilarity: bad acting, lazy writing, and poorly rendered CGI effects. Much of the cast spends their time alternating between giving badly timed, underwhelming line reads and "showing emotion" by screaming at the top of their lungs. This isn't helped by the script, which is appropriate for a B-movie titled *Mega Piranha*, but is far from inspired.

The CGI piranhas are the biggest highlight though, and will have you rolling on the floor throughout the movie. It can't be easy to make an elephant-sized piranha look realistic, but it cer- tainly isn't helped when you constantly allow your fish to change size and perform ridiculous stunts. For instance, there's one scene in which Fitch is laying on his back on the beach and is attacked by a series of piranhas jumping out of the water. They come at him one after the other while he bicycle kicks them away in a scene that's hilarious, only because it's so stupidly implausible.

The ending to *Mega Piranha* is just as implausible as the rest of the film, but you'll have long stopped caring by that point. This is pure low-budget monster/disaster movie fun, and serves as a great introduction for what The Asylum has to offer. If you have a good time with this movie, you might also want to check out a few of their other movies—*The 7 Adventures of Sinbad* (famous for its crab battle scene) and *Sherlock Holmes* (in which Holmes battles a robotic dinosaur in Victorian era London) are among my favorites.

COOL AS ICE
DIRECTED BY DAVID KELLOGG
ALIVE FILMS, CAPELLA, KOPPELMANN/
BANDIER-CARNEIGE PICTURES (1991)

One of the more infamous flops in recent memory, *Cool as Ice* is a romantic comedy starring Vanilla Ice. Do I even need to write a summary for you to understand why this is a movie you need to watch?

If you must know more, Vanilla Ice plays—get this—a rapper named Johnny Van Owen. He and his posse travel around on motorcycles, so when one of the bikes breaks down, that leaves Johnny and the crew stuck in a small town until it can be repaired. That's where Johnny meets Kathy Winslow (Kristen Minter), an honor student who would never have anything to do with a ruffian like Johnny...or would she?

The romance in *Cool as Ice* is remarkably cliché, making sure to hit all of the plot points you'd expect. Kathy has a boyfriend, Nick (John Newton), who is from her social class, but treats her badly, leading the audience to once again wonder why she ever dated him in the first place. Through a series of romantic gestures, Johnny manages to show Kathy that he's not just some loser—he's a rapper with a heart of gold. Somewhere in the middle of all this, Vanilla Ice gets to deliver what has become the signature line of this film: "Drop that zero and get with the hero!"

If romance isn't your thing, Ice has you covered, because this film managed to shoehorn in some action. It turns out that Kathy's father, Gordon (Michael Gross), is actually on the run from some corrupt cops who have now managed to track him and his family down. They manage to kidnap Kathy's younger brother, Tommy, leading Gordon to accuse Johnny of having some sort of involvement.

Johnny exonerates himself in fine fashion, first by playing detective to figure out where Tommy is being held, then by mounting a rescue operation with the help of his gang. If you've ever wanted to see Vanilla Ice on a motorcycle flying into houses or jumping over cars, this is your chance!

As I said earlier, this movie wasn't a hit at the box office, though just how badly it did was pretty shocking. *Cool as Ice* had a budget of only six million dollars, and still managed to come nowhere near recouping that in theaters, bringing in less than 1.2 million in ticket sales. This happened when Vanilla Ice was a legitimate star. The complete failure of the film may have been a sign that he was overexposed and was likely to have a limited shelf life.

Of course, it didn't help that the movie was absolutely terrible. The plot is ridiculous, the editing tries way too hard to be "cool" through the use of random fast-forwarding and cuts to Ice doing random activities like laying down on a couch, and if the musical numbers scattered throughout the film were designed to show us how talented he was as a rapper, you can count that among the movie's many failings. Still, if you're going to fail, it's best to fail spectacularly: as far as bad movie fans are concerned, *Cool as Ice* was an unqualified success.

BEN & ARTHUR
DIRECTED BY SAM MRAOVICH
SAM MRAOVICH PRODUCTIONS (2002)

If your film has a message, it's usually a fair bet that someone will like it. After all, even if your production values are lacking, the acting is terrible, and you're not a particularly gifted film-maker, those who feel your message is important are likely to overlook these issues.

On the surface, *Ben & Arthur* would appear to be such a film. It tackles the heated topic of gay marriage, following the couple of Ben Sheets (Jamie Brett Gabel) and Arthur Sailes (Sam Mraovich) as they hope to have their relationship recognized by the state of California. It's a movie that—especially at the time it was made—explored a relationship that was rarely seen in film, and while the message is certainly contentious, support for the rights of same-sex couples in the United States was already growing stronger in 2002, and continues to do so to this day.

So Bad, It's Good

So where does it all go wrong? Well, it turns out that this isn't just a simple story of a gay couple fighting for their right to marry. As the film proceeds, we're introduced to Ben's brother, Victor (Michael Haboush), a devout Christian who is firmly against his brother's sexuality, and wants to "cure" him through the power of prayer—and secret holy water recipes. This is the kind of conflict you'd expect to find in this movie, so no surprises there.

What does come as a shock is just how far Victor is willing to go in his efforts and just how strongly his church feels about the issue. When Victor's priest finds out about Ben, Victor is expelled from the church for having a gay brother. Victor's response isn't to find a new church, but rather to work with the priest in an attempt to arrange Ben's murder. Now, while it's certainly true that many Christians have deep oppositions to gay marriage, and that many of these same people hold homophobic beliefs, I'm going to go out on a limb and say that even this subgroup isn't accurately represented by the characters in *Ben & Arthur*.

While the film has a clear bias, don't let that fool you: our heroes do plenty of reprehensible things themselves. In revenge for the attempted murder of Ben, Arthur does some investigation of his own, and manages to fool the priest into giving him the information he needs in order to find Victor. That's a reasonable—and clever—thing to do. Less reasonable is Arthur's decision to knock out the priest and burn down his church, surely killing him and anyone else who happened to be inside. Oops!

Ben & Arthur is clearly a low-budget, independent film, and the production values make this clear—though to be fair, it's largely free of the kinds of blatant editing issues or laughable effects seen in films like *Birdemic*. This movie was largely a one-man effort, with Mraovich not only taking on a leading role, but also writing, directing, and producing—he's credited as both the producer and the executive producer—the film, as well as being heavily involved in creating the music for the film.

Regardless of how you feel about the issues presented in this movie, you're likely to find something in *Ben & Arthur* that offends you—and if you love bad movies, you should still go out of your way to find a copy and watch it. *Ben & Arthur* has been called "the worst gay movie of all time," and at the time of this writing, is ranked at #5 in the IMDB Bottom 100. I wouldn't quite rank it that highly, but as long as you can shut off the part of your brain that takes these very serious issues so seriously for a couple of hours, it is certainly one of the most enjoyably terrible films ever made.

NO HOLDS BARRED
DIRECTED BY THOMAS J. WRIGHT
NEW LINE CINEMA (1989)

Hulk Hogan turned the World Wrestling Federation from a major player in professional wrestling to one of the biggest entertainment brands in the world. I'm not the most knowledgeable wrestling fan, but I take it that Hogan was never the greatest worker in the ring. Instead, it was his undeniable charisma and his ability to fire up crowds that turned him into the legendary face of professional wrestling.

With that kind of pedigree, one would expect that Hogan would easily transition over to the world of feature films. This is the part where you'd expect me to make a joke about how badly he failed as an actor, but I'll cut the guy a little slack. Sure, he won't be winning any Oscars for his work, but he's usually only required to play a version of himself, and for the most part, he can handle that.

No Holds Barred is a perfect example of Hulk playing Hulk. In 1982, Hogan had a small role in *Rocky III*, playing a professional wrestler named Thunderlips who fought Rocky Balboa in a charity exhibition. That was enough to convince WWF executives that Hogan could probably carry his own film franchise. In 1989, Hulkamania was at its peak, and this seemed like the perfect time to launch wrestling's biggest star onto the big screen.

In *No Holds Barred*, Hogan plays—you guessed it—a professional wrestler named Rip. He's a hero who is beloved by fans, and is an even better guy away from the camera. He's even a great guy away from the ring, where he's actively involved in charitable work while remaining close to his younger brother, Randy. In other words, there's really no reason why you shouldn't be rooting for this guy.

But there is one man who doesn't love Rip. Professional wrestling is so popular that it is killing the ratings of a rival network, which is headed by Brell (Kurt Fuller). Seeing the popularity of bar brawls with no rules, Brell decides that he can get his network back on top by starting his own brand of wrestling known as "Battle of the Tough Guys," which is quite possibly the worst name ever for a wrestling program. The new show is immediately popular, but is put over the top by the introduction of Zeus (Tom Lister, Jr.), a monstrously strong and vicious competitor who appears to be unbeatable.

At this point, it's pretty clear what all this is heading to, but we still have a few subplots to get out of the way first. Rip has to deal with a corporate spy (Joan Severance), who he manages to win over with his kindhearted ways. Brell and Zeus terrorize Rip and his family in an attempt to get him to fight Zeus on Battle of the Tough Guys.

Eventually, the two get into the ring together, and wouldn't you know it: things look bad for our hero. Can Rip overcome the odds and defeat his nemesis? I think you already know the answer. Just in case this wasn't enough for wrestling fans, the WWF also set up a pay-per-view feud that culminated in a tag team, steel cage match that features Hulk Hogan and Zeus on opposite sides.

No Holds Barred is goofy, but it's also a lot of fun. All of the scenes in which the executives of the rival network are hanging around in dive bars are simply surreal, watching cheesy villains get their comeuppance never gets old, and the wrestling set pieces—of which there are plenty—deliver pretty much what you expect them to. The Hulkster tries his best to take it all seriously, though he's definitely better when he's asked to be a wrestler than when he's attempting to show his range as an actor. All told, this is the perfect bad movie for anyone who misses the days when Hulk Hogan and Andre the Giant ruled the world.

CHOPPING MALL
DIRECTED BY JIM WYNORSKI
CONCORDE PICTURES, TRINITY PICTURES
(1986)

Some puns are too good not to use. I have to assume that was the inspiration behind *Chopping Mall*, the film that used the brilliant tag line of "where shopping can cost you an arm and a leg." It's not the original title of the film—that would be *Killbots*—but it's not surprising that the film did much better after the name change. While the movie does feature robots that kill, *Chopping Mall* is the kind of name that's going to draw in B-movie aficionados with no further explanation necessary.

The film is about Park Plaza Mall, a shopping center that has recently decided to try something a little different when it comes to security. Move aside, *Paul Blart, Mall Cop*—Park Plaza is bringing in three security robots that have been programmed to disable and detain criminals while the mall is closed overnight.

In a stunning coincidence, the first time that these robots are on the job also happens to be the night when four couples have decided to throw a party in a furniture store. And wouldn't you know it, a lightning strike causes a malfunction in the security robots, causing them to go from detaining thieves to killing anyone they encounter.

What follows is your standard horror movie plot progression. One couple leaves the furniture store in search of cigarettes, providing the robots with their first kills. From there, the survivors battle with the robot menace, using their wits and any weapons they can find to try and survive the night. A mall is a great location for a setup like this, as it provides our heroes with plenty of ways to get their hands on helpful materials—guns are scavenged from a sporting goods store and flammable materials are abundant.

Chopping Mall is a delightful example of 1980s cheese. There's your standard cast of nerds and jocks, the theme music is played on a synthesizer, and everything from the robots to the mall itself features that modern 80s aesthetic. Filmed on a tight budget, the effects aren't exactly terrible, but you'll still get to enjoy a nice combination of robots firing laser weapons and exploding heads. You'll also have fun wondering why the robots' tactics and ability to hit a target standing a few feet in front of them vary depending on the needs of the plot.

At a very manageable running time of seventy-seven minutes, *Chopping Mall* has the good sense to wrap things up before the viewer gets tired of watching Cylon-like robots hunt down annoying teenagers. While it's certainly stupid, this movie delivers plenty of nostalgic fun, and is worth checking out if you're a fan of bad horror movies.

MAZES AND MONSTERS
DIRECTED BY STEVEN HILLIARD STERN
MCDERMOTT PRODUCTIONS, PROCTER &
GAMBLE PRODUCTIONS (1982)

In today's world, *Dungeons & Dragons* is seen as a role-playing game that is mainly played by dedicated tabletop gamers who tend to be a bit on the nerdy and socially awkward side. But in the early 1980s, *D&D* was viewed by the public as a role-playing game that was mainly played by dedicated tabletop games who tended to be a bit on the nerdy and socially awkward side...that could lead children into the arms of Satan himself. Yes, the classic game of wizards and warriors, elves and dwarves, went through a period of time when it was vilified by some religious groups for supposedly encouraging occult activity. Actually, there are still those that maintain that link exists to this day and *D&D* isn't the only entity that has weathered such attacks—to a lesser extent, games like *Magic: The Gathering* would see similar charges levied against them into the 1990s, and most readers are probably familiar with those who accuse the *Harry Potter* series of books of introducing children to the evils of magic.

Still, the effort to paint *D&D* as an evil and dangerous game was never stronger than in the early 1980s, and it's that environment that produced the television movie *Mazes and Monsters*. The movie is based on a book of the same name, which was in turn based on the tale of James Egbert III, a Michigan State University student who disappeared in 1979. In the wake of the disappearance, early media reports suggested that Egbert disappeared in steam tunnels near campus during a live action role-playing session. In reality, this was just a theory advanced by a private investigator that had been mistakenly reported as fact. Egbert had actually run away from campus of his own accord, and though he had entered the steam tunnels, it had nothing to do with gaming—it was part of an attempted suicide. Sadly, Egbert would eventually take his life almost exactly a year later.

But quick cash-in novels can't wait for the truth to come out. Author Rona Jaffe didn't want to wait for someone else to beat her to the punch. She quickly wrote a fictionalized account of the Egbert story, based on the initial accounts that featured *D&D* as a contributing factor in his death. This was the story that would ultimately become a CBS television movie in 1982.

The film is about college student Robbie Wheeling (Tom Hanks). Yes, Tom Hanks' career as a film star began here (though he already had a leading role in the television series *Bosom Buddies*). Robbie is attending Grant University in the hopes of furthering his education and getting over the disappearance of his brother, Hall.

Robbie is also a former player of the game *Mazes and Monsters*, which is essentially *D&D* without the need to pay for the rights to use the game's name in the movie. While he initially has no plans to play the game in college—he previously flunked out of a different university due to playing too much—Robbie soon makes friends who persuade him to round out their gaming group. There's obligatory love interest, Kate (Wendy Crewson), fifteen-year-old child prodigy, Jay Jay (Chris Makepeace), who wears strange hats, and aspiring video game designer, Daniel (David Wallace). The four play together and the games go on without incident.

For Robbie, college is going quite well. He and Kate start dating, and unlike in his past experiences, he's managed to balance gaming and schoolwork. On the other hand, Jay Jay decides he wants to create a stir by killing himself in a nearby cavern. But upon seeing just how intricate and beautiful the caves are, he changes his mind and decides to host a live action *Mazes and Monsters* game for the group.

So far, the story seems vaguely like the supposed Egbert disappearance, but here's where things really start to go off track. After playing a game in the caverns, Robbie has some sort of psychotic breakdown and begins to believe he's actually his character, a cleric named Pardeux. It takes his friends a surprisingly long time to realize the depth of the issue, considering Robbie walks around campus blessing his classmates and breaking up with Kate in order to honor his vow of celibacy.

From there, Robbie's life spirals out of control as his alter ego searches for his missing brother. This leads him to New York City, where he casts magic spells and kills muggers. His friends eventually track him down for a climax that is among the most ridiculous you'll see in any thriller. That's followed by a denouement that seems designed to teach us that *D&D* players can be damaged beyond repair with no hope of ever recovering—what a lovely message.

Mazes and Monsters is an amazing look at an era of gaming that many current *D&D* players are far too young to remember. While the movie is absurd to modern audiences, try to watch it with the knowledge that at least some portion of those who saw it when it aired took this as an accurate portrayal of role-playing games and the people who played them. This movie is ridiculous enough to please any audience, but it's a must-watch for serious gamers who want to know exactly what 1982 thought about them.

ABSOLUTE ZERO
DIRECTED BY ROBERT LEE
FRONT STREET PICTURES, THINKFILM, ZERO STREET PRODUCTIONS (2006)

Disaster movies have always enjoyed some popularity, but starting in the 1990s, the number of "end of the world" films began to increase exponentially. It seemed as though every week, there was a new threat to our planet: an asteroid, earthquakes, volcanoes, and aliens all took their turns nearly ending our fragile existence.

Absolute Zero is yet another of these films. Released in 2006, it uses climate change as the impending disaster, which by that point had become the most popular way for filmmakers to kill off millions of human beings in one fell swoop. Interestingly, this film doesn't actually use global warming as the means for a climate disaster. It gets a mention, but the plot quickly goes off in a completely different—and much stupider—direction.

Our main character is David Koch (Jeff Fahey), a climate scientist who works for a company known as Inter Sci. Over the course of the film, he works with two of his student assistants to come up with a theory that ice ages are actually caused by polar shifts caused by geomagnetic reversal. They then find evidence that these shifts don't take place gradually over the course of thousands of years, as scientists believe, but instead happen in a single day. In addition, he believes that the polarity will shift only halfway, leaving both poles at the equator—and that it could happen at any moment. That's admittedly a lot to swallow, and his former boss Dr. Veet (Bill Dow) strongly opposes these findings, saying that his massive team of scientists doesn't expect any polar shift to occur for hundreds of years.

If you've ever watched a disaster movie before, you can probably figure out who ends up being right. Things start going wrong in Miami—and presumably other places, though we never see that, as the majority of the film takes place in the city—as news reports tell us of birds migrating months earlier than normal and a large iceberg finds its way into the city's harbor.

Why that happens before temperatures actually drop is the least of the scientific issues with *Absolute Zero*. One of the most quotable lines from the movie—repeated by a couple of different characters—is that "science is never wrong." It's not really clear whether the film wants us to believe this—in a "well-done science is an ongoing process that seeks to reach objectively correct conclusions" manner—or mock it—"look at those silly scientists, they didn't know the magnetic poles would move to the equator somehow!" But that doesn't matter. When dealing with what happens in this movie, it's much easier to assume that the science is *never* right.

When disaster ultimately strikes, temperatures rapidly drop in Miami, as well as everywhere else near the equator—up to about thirty degrees north and south. For some reason that's never adequately explained, this doesn't just make the formerly tropical regions of the world cold, but actually drops the temperature to absolute zero, or about negative two hundred and seventy-three Celsius (negative four hundred and sixty Fahrenheit). You don't have to be a scientist to understand that a lot of things would be quite different at that temperature: little things, like the complete lack of most forms of energy, might make surviving such a change rather difficult. It's also entirely impossible to reach such a state naturally, and certainly not on a planet with an atmosphere, living beings, a molten core, and a sun.

To be fair, not all scientific inaccuracies are equally damaging to the enjoyment of a film. While most of us would like the movies we watch to remain internally consistent and vaguely plausible, smaller mistakes can be forgiven. With that in mind, let's take a look at a couple of the mistakes or errors made in *Absolute Zero* with an eye on better understanding what's okay and what's not. The IMDB page for this movie lists several "factual errors," including the following:

- The university professor states that the Earth's atmosphere is seventy-nine percent Nitrogen. In fact it is only seventy-eight percent Nitrogen.

This is an understandable error that anyone could make. On the other hand:

- Once absolute zero is attained, all gases and liquids should be in solid states. Also, most gases liquefy a hundred degrees before absolute zero, thus the Earth should have became flooded, then once absolute zero was attained, everything should have been solid.

Well, that's a bit harder to swallow.

Without a doubt, *Absolute Zero* is one of the stupider disaster movies out there, which is saying something for a genre that isn't known for its cerebral nature. In this case, though, that's part of the fun, as the ludicrous premise will have you constantly screaming at the screen and wondering how physics works in this movie's universe. Remember, science is never wrong, but movie science is always open for mockery.

More Recommendations

If you asked one hundred fans of terrible cinema for their opinions on what the best "so bad, it's good" movie is, you'd likely get close to one hundred different answers, each of which has something to offer. I can't begin to claim that I have the final knowledge on what films make for the best bad movie viewing experiences, so I reached out to the community for a few more suggestions. Below, you'll find the picks of several fans and critics alike—any of which would make a fine selection for your next bad movie night.

BLOOD DINER
DIRECTED BY JACKIE KONG
PMS FILMWORKS, VESTRON PICTURES (1987)

The horror/comedy genre has produced a number of excellent movies as well as plenty of bad films that are a lot of fun to watch. There's always the danger that these movies become a little bit too self-aware: sometimes, a movie isn't just trying to be

125

funny, but becomes a parody of itself, essentially falling into the trap of being bad on purpose. The key is finding a movie that strikes the right balance of intentional laughs that don't come at the expense of the film along with unintentional cheese that will have you laughing for all the wrong reasons.

One movie that strikes the perfect note in this regard is *Blood Diner*, the 1987 film about two brothers who take instructions from their dead serial killer uncle—they have his brain and penis in a jar—who wants them to resurrect an ancient goddess.

"It seems to know exactly how crazy, stupid, goofy, and weird it is," says James "Crypticpsych" Lasome, who writes for Best-Horror-Movies.com, "and it embraces that fact wholeheartedly, and is actually more crazy, insane, and endearing for it. It's just moment after moment of unforgettable scenes and instant classic moments."

STARSHIP TROOPERS 3: MARAUDER
DIRECTED BY EDWARD NEUMEIER
SONG PICTURES HOME ENTERTAINMENT,
APOLLOMOVIE BETEILIGUNGS, BOLD FILMS,
FILM AFRIKA WORLDWIDE (2008)

Starship Troopers 3: Marauder was a direct-to-DVD release that brought back Johnny Rico (Casper Van Dien), the hero of the first film in the series. The movie chronicles Rico's continuing adventures in the war against the arachnids as he leads a rescue mission on a classified planet that's secretly the home of The Brain of Brains—leader and god of the entire bug civilization. While the original *Starship Troopers* was undeniably campy and fun, bad movie fan Andrew Joyce says that this installment takes those elements to a whole new level.

"It's a campfest movie that knows it is...but still tries to be serious with its plot," Joyce says. "It takes all of the amusing campiness of the first film and turns it up to eleven, then adds in religion: not just for the humans, but for the bugs, too. It's an enjoyable watch from start to finish."

UNDEFEATABLE
DIRECTED BY GODFREY HO
WHE EUROPE LIMITED (1993)

If you're a fan of martial arts movies, you'll have no trouble finding dozens, perhaps even hundreds, of enjoyably cheesy films filled with non-stop action. A few of these movies manage to stand out from the crowd, and *Undefeatable* is one of the greatest examples of all. I've seen the film myself, but other than the climactic fight scene—which is infamous in its own right—I can't claim to be an expert on this Cynthia Rothrock classic. Instead, I'll leave this one to Allison Pregler, who reviewed *Undefeatable* in the first ever episode of *Obscurus Lupa Presents*. In her own words:

What can I say about *Undefeatable*? It was the first "so bad, it's good" movie I ever saw. It helped set me on my current career path reviewing enjoyably bad films. And, perhaps most important of all, it introduced me to the fantastic Cynthia Rothrock.

First, let me say this: the fact this film exists is pretty amazing. It was directed by Godfrey Ho, who was infamous for filming footage of Caucasian actors to splice into old ninja movies and sell in the American market. However, he actually filmed two movies in America (*Undefeatable* and another hilarious feature called *Honor and Glory*) and spliced in footage of Asian actors to sell in that market, effectively reversing his process. It's a fascinating look at how he made movies. It also explains a bit of why the film turned out like it did, because Ho was using different movie-making sensibilities in creating this feature. The dialogue is stilted, the situations are silly, and the acting is amazingly bad. Some of it is lost in translation, but a lot of it is just good old-fashioned martial arts glory. If you like cheese-tastic villains, stiff heroes, and some serviceable action scenes—including the infamous final fight—it's worth checking this movie out.

THE MARINE
DIRECTED BY JOHN BONITO
WWE FILMS, TWENTIETH CENTURY FOX,
PACIFIC FILM AND TELEVISION COMMISSION
(2006)

World Wrestling Entertainment has long tried to market its top stars in feature films, going back to the days when it was called the World Wrestling Federation and Hulk Hogan was their most famous face. Most of these films have been poorly received by critics and *The Marine* is no exception to this rule.

John Cena stars as the titular Marine, a hero named John Triton who has been honorably discharged from the Marine Corps after saving several of his fellow soldiers. Back at home, his wife is kidnapped by jewelry thieves on the run from the police. For the rest of the film, Triton tracks down the thieves in an attempt to save his wife.

This film was brought to my attention by bad movie fan Patrick Alexander, who calls *The Marine* one of the funniest movies he's ever seen.

"John Cena's attempts to act, his no-selling fire and a fire extinguisher to the face, a random subplot about rock candy, the moronic score," Alexander told me, listing just a few of the many faults in this film. "I could go on about how laughably incompetent it is for days."

KILLER KLOWNS FROM OUTER SPACE
DIRECTED BY STEPHEN CHIODO
CHIODO BROTHERS PRODUCTIONS, SARLUI/
DIAMANT (1988)

If you can't get enough of horror/comedy crossovers, *Killer Klowns from Outer Space* is one of the classics of the genre. It's something like an updated version of a 1950s B-movie, with a plot that involves aliens—who look like evil clowns, and who pilot a spaceship that looks like the big top tent of a carnival or circus—invading Earth in order to harvest human beings as a food source.

Strictly speaking, many film buffs don't think of *Killer Klowns* as a bad film, but it's certainly the kind of film that bad movie aficionados appreciate. As fan Douglas Fox points out, it has the kind of charm you simply can't get from a big-budget Hollywood production.

"You can tell the movie was made with a lot of love and they had a ton of fun making it," Fox says. "They didn't spend money on sets, actors, or a script, just makeup and special effects. It's a movie I am proud to own."

Honorable (and Dishonorable) Mentions

The creation of this book required me to watch a lot of bad movies. Plenty of these movies were a lot of fun to watch and were obvious inclusions in this book, while others—for one reason or another—didn't quite seem to fit. Some were just plain bad, a few had something about them that didn't make them quite right for the book, and others just weren't quite up to par in my eyes—though others clearly loved watching them.

For these and any number of other reasons, I was left with a list of films that were interesting for one reason or another, but weren't going to make the book. It seemed like a waste to have spent hours watching these movies and not even mention them, though, so I've added a list here of some other films worth taking a look at. Below, you'll find brief descriptions of each of these films, as well as a short explanation as to why I didn't include each in the main body of this book. Each of these movies is at least worth considering: you might just find a couple that make your bad movie rotation.

THE LOST SKELETON OF CADAVRA
DIRECTED BY LARRY BLAMIRE
FRAGMIGHTY, TRANSOM FILMS, VALENTI
ENTERTAINMENT (2004)
AND
THE LOST SKELETON RETURNS AGAIN
DIRECTED BY LARRY BLAMIRE
BANTAM STREET (2009)

Both of the *Lost Skeleton* films are favorites among bad movie fans. However, they don't quite belong in a book about bad movies because...well, they're not actually bad. These films spoof the B-movies of the 1950s, and do a brilliant job of paying homage to the campiness of that era. Made on small budgets, these movies are intentionally campy: they feature hokey dialogue, wooden performances, and recycled props, all of which help to capture the feel of a classic B-movie. Both movies are filled with continuity errors and terrible effects, but that's all part of the show—which makes the *Lost Skeleton* series great to watch, but also means that they're not the kind of bad movies this book is all about.

If the concept is one that intrigues you, you'll be happy to know that there are more Larry Blamire films the fit this same mold. *Trail of the Screaming Forehead* is just as fun as the *Lost Skeleton* movies, as is *Dark and Stormy Night,* a parody of 1930s murder mysteries and haunted house stories. Finally, if you want more *Lost Skeleton* adventures, you're in luck: a third film in the series—*The Lost Skeleton Walks Among Us*—is currently in development.

VALOR'S KIDS
DIRECTED BY KAI MARIAH
SOMEWHERE OVER THE RAINBOW
PRODUCTIONS (2011)

I love *Valor's Kids*. It's a CGI fantasy film with hilariously bad animation, a plot that's circuitous and rather inconsequential to your enjoyment of the movie, and voice acting that could charitably be called amateurish. In fact, I've watched this film several times with different audiences, and we have never, ever failed to have a good time.

In short, *Valor's Kids* is perfect for this book, except for one thing: The director wasn't quite twelve-years-old when she started working on the film. I don't know about you, but I feel a little weird about publically mocking the work of a teenager—she finished the movie at the ripe old age of fifteen—especially since simply completing a film and getting it distributed in even a very limited fashion is quite an accomplishment at that age.

But none of that takes away from the fact that you'll have a blast watching this movie, if you can get your hands on it. Only a very limited number of DVDs were ever produced, and it's unlikely that you'll be able to find one now. However, digital copies are available through the website NewFilmmakersOnline.com. If you want to see one of the truly great bad movies out there, purchase a copy. You'll be encouraging a young filmmaker to further their craft, which might absolve you of any guilt you feel when laughing at her work. Once the film begins, sit back and enjoy the fun. I'm certain that you've never see anything remotely like *Valor's Kids* before.

TIPTOES
DIRECTED BY MATTHEW BRIGHT
LANGLEY PRODUCTIONS, MARSHAK/ ZACHARY, CANAL+, STUDIO CANAL, WILD BUNCH (2003)

Tiptoes is a bizarre film that could easily have earned a place in this book. However, I, and many of my viewing companions, found the movie to be more "so bad, it's stupid" than "so bad, it's good." The plot follows Steven (Matthew McConaughey) and Carol (Kate Beckinsale), a young couple that could be on the verge of marriage. No matter how hard Carol presses, though, Steven won't tell her about his family—and when she becomes pregnant, Steven becomes especially worried and elusive.

Before long, Carol finds out the secret that Steven has been hiding: his entire family is made up of dwarves (except for Steven, who happened to avoid the genetic condition). The question then becomes whether Carol and Steven can accept the fact that their child might very well be a dwarf as well. In the real world, the answer would certainly be yes. In *Tiptoes*, both parents take turns being uncertain about this.

This movie has an excellent cast, including David Alan Grier, Patricia Arquette, and Peter Dinklage—who plays Maurice, a French Marxist dwarf who's just waiting for the revolution to come. But the most absurd casting in this film is that of Steven's brother Rolfe, who is played by none other than Gary Oldman—"in the role of a lifetime," according to the trailer. If you're wondering how Oldman plays a dwarf, his technique is rather simple: it appears as though he just walks around on his knees for the entire film. This leads to plenty of scenes where Oldman either looks to be the wrong size or wrong proportion when compared to the many characters portrayed by actors and actresses who actually are dwarves—and it's all played completely straight.

Tiptoes could have been a movie that explored important and difficult issues in a serious manner, but most of the time, it simply doesn't work. There are certainly parts of the movie that are enjoyably cheesy, but mostly, it's more of a failed serious movie than an enjoyably bad one, despite how promising the concept might seem. Still, it has its moments, so if the idea of Gary Oldman pretending to be a little person makes you giggle, you might want to check it out.

AFTER LAST SEASON
DIRECTED BY MARK REGION
INDEX SPARE (2009)

After Last Season is something of legendary bad movie. You can't find a Wikipedia article on it, and if you come across a copy on eBay or Amazon, you'd better scoop it up before it's gone forever. As far as I can tell, it seems as though the creators of the film would be happy to pretend it never existed.

Trying to describe *After Last Season* is an exercise in futility, and it's difficult to come up with a way to summarize it. The two main characters are medical students and interns at the Prorolis Corporation, which is supposedly developing technology that allows one person to see into another's mind. It's unclear how, or if, this relates to the other main plot, which involves a series of unsolved murders. There's also a ghost who throws chairs at people.

Incredibly, the plot may be one of the least problematic aspects of the movie. Poor acting is almost a given in a movie such as this, but the actors weren't given any help by the script. Characters go on and on about where they used to live and what towns they've been through. Doctors take a few minutes at a time to explain machines, tests, and results to other doctors, who should already be familiar with this material. During a phone call, one character tells another that a building has printers they can use in the basement. Here's a sample from late in the film that makes about as much sense as anything else you'll hear: "My husband spotted a coyote near that tree. It stood there for several seconds, then went away." Don't worry, context doesn't help.

Then there's the set design. Most of the film takes place in a series of sparsely occupied rooms that look like they could have all come from the same house. Throughout the film, walls are covered with blank white paper—which may or may not have been an attempt at some sort of artistic statement. There's an MRI machine that's clearly made out of cardboard. Sometimes, there's wallpaper that covers only a small portion of a wall.

A fair potion of the film takes place when one character is looking into the mind of the other. These scenes are completely CGI, as the "viewer" sees the "geometric shapes" that are floating around the other character's mind. The result is something that more-or-less resembles a screensaver from Windows 95.

After Last Season probably sounds like a perfect candidate for bad movie night, and with the right crowd, it might be. But getting through the full ninety minutes is a bit of a challenge, and it's quite possible that people will be pleading with you to give in and put on something more sensible—like *Pocket Ninjas*—before they go insane. Some of your friends will likely believe that this movie was made to be bad on purpose, but all available evidence points to the contrary. It's hard to even say that it's a bad movie, because it's difficult to be certain that it should be classified as a movie at all. Whatever it is, there's no doubt that *After Last Season* is fascinating, bizarre, and somehow both incredibly dull and impossibly intriguing at the same time. Now that you've read this, I'm sure you'll try to find a copy. Go ahead and watch it—but don't say you weren't warned.

DÜNYAYI KURTARAN ADAM (THE MAN WHO SAVED THE WORLD) DIRECTED BY ÇETIN İNANÇ ANIT FILM (1982) AND ÖLÜM SAVAŞÇISI (DEATH WARRIOR) DIRECTED BY ÇETIN İNANÇ AND CÜNEYT ARKIN BIRINCI TICARETIM (1984)

Over the last few years, badly subtitled versions of some foreign films have become a popular part of the bad movie lexicon. Sure, movies from China and Japan have long been popular—particularly when it comes to martial arts movies—but these days it is possible to find movies from just about anywhere.

Some of the most popular movies of this type—at least among bad movie fans—are 1980s era films from Turkey, many of which use footage "borrowed" from more popular Hollywood films. For instance, *The Man Who Saved the World* liberally uses footage from *Star Wars*, though the plot is almost entirely unrelated to George Lucas' work. Similarly, *Death Warrior* uses plenty of music and sounds from *The Thing*.

What makes these movies so much fun? I'd say they offer over-the-top action, but that's shortchanging just how insane the action scenes can get, with our hero (played by Cüneyt Arkin, a legitimate film star, in both movies) using his extensive martial arts skills to battle thugs, ninjas, monsters, aliens, and anything else that has been thrown in his way. Everything is deliciously low-budget, from the stock sound effects and natural sets to the special effects that combine practical effects with film trickery to create a uniquely Turkish aesthetic. The plots are thin and mostly exist to set up plenty of action scenes for our hero.

I couldn't fully recommend these films, primarily because there are a lot of viewers who won't be able to get into them, and many more that will enjoy watching one of these movies a single time, but will quickly become less interested after that. Again, this is another movie that would work with the right audience, but probably isn't the best way to introduce prospective fans into the world of bad movies, and might not work well with a general audience.

THE ROLLER BLADE SEVEN
DIRECTED BY DONALD G. JACKSON
THE REBEL CORP. (1991)
AND
MAX HELL FROG WARRIOR
DIRECTED BY DONALD G. JACKSON AND
SCOTT SHAW LIGHT SOURCE FILMS (2002)

The team of Scott Shaw and Donald G. Jackson are responsible for the concept known as "Zen Filmmaking," something they have used on several of their combined projects, including the two listed here. In a nutshell, Zen Filmmaking is a free-form style of movie creation that doesn't rely on scripts and instead focuses on making virtually all decisions spontaneously as situations allow for. There are few or no sets, actors are only given a general sense of what should happen in each scene, and the directors choose to work with whatever they get when they film, good or bad. Perhaps two quotes about the tenets of Zen Filmmaking from Scott Shaw's own website can sum up the process best:

- "Just do it! Ninety-nine percent of the time you can get away with it."
- "Ultimately, in Zen Filmmaking nothing is desired and, thus, all outcomes are perfect."

As you might imagine, the end result is something much different that you'd get from the traditional filmmaking process. Without the constraints of scripts or the desire to do re-shoots, the quality of a Zen film can vary from shot to shot, and there's never a guarantee of a coherent plot from start to finish. In many cases, the director may not care if there's a story at all.

The two films listed here are among the best-known examples of Zen Filmmaking. In *The Roller Blade Seven*, Hawk Goodman (Scott Shaw) must rescue the kidnapped Sister Sparrow from villains—including Saint Offender (Joe Estevez) and the Black Knight (Frank Stallone)—all in a post-apocalyptic world where everyone travels around on skateboards and rollerblades. *Max Hell Frog Warrior* follows Max Hell (Scott Shaw) who needs to rescue the kidnapped Dr. Trixi T (Elizabeth Mehr) from the villainous Mickey O'Malley (Joe Estevez).

Many bad movie fans will want to check at least one of these films out, if only to get a better idea of what exactly Zen Filmmaking is. On the other hand, the style can quickly become grating instead of fun, as you'll have to endure long periods where it feels like virtually nothing is happening on screen. There are also numerous instances in which shots are repeated or footage is reused—something that is amusing when you first notice it, but which can quickly get tiresome. Zen Filmmaking definitely isn't for everyone, and I'd recommend checking out a small sample before deciding to watch an entire movie in this style.

Finding More Movies

If you've been intrigued by the movies included in this book, but want to find more "so bad, they're good" films to enjoy, the internet offers plenty of resources that can point you in the right direction. Here are a few of my favorites:

- A great starting point is the Internet Movie Database (IMDB), which I've referred to throughout this book. They allow users to rate essentially every film ever made, and more importantly, keep a Bottom 100 list that ranks the lowest-rated films in their database. There are also bottom lists by genre if you have a particular type of movie you're looking for. Combine that with an easy to navigate site that can easily help you find other films starring a director or actor you enjoy and IMDB makes it quick and easy to find dozens of great bad movies.
- If you'd like to get expert opinions on which bad movies you should watch, there are numerous individuals online who produce video reviews of all kinds of movies— from new releases to forgotten classics. One of the best

collections of such reviews is That Guy with the Glasses, a site that employs several movie reviewers—among others who review games, comics, and more—who host web shows that look at films every week. Many of these shows routinely look at movies that could be—or are—in this book. Some of the best for bad movie fans include *The Nostalgia Critic, Bad Movie Beatdown, Obscurus Lupa Presents,* and *The Cinema Snob,* as well as the reviews by Phelous (Phelan Porteous).

- Another great resource is BadMovies.org. This website has reviewed hundreds of B-movies, ranging from the extremely entertaining to the incredibly painful. They're also regularly adding more reviews from the site, so it's a great place to dig for cinematic treasure.

Made in the USA
Lexington, KY
11 December 2012